Dale L. Shelly
P.O. Box 6070
Wyomissing, PA 19610
www.dalescookbook.com

Original Wild Game, Fish, and Seafood Recipes

Copyright © 2000 Dale L. Shelly

Second Edition

Dale L. Shelly

Printed by
Sir Speedy
PRINTING • COPYING • DIGITAL NETWORK
West Lawn, PA

CONTENTS

FOREWARD

All my life, I have enjoyed hunting and fishing. I have especially enjoyed preparing my bounty (and also the fish and game given to me by friends) into favorite recipes I developed over the years, and sharing them with friends and relatives.

On numerous occasions, individuals would ask for recipes of certain dishes and so with this cookbook, I attempted to gather my efforts all together in one place. Since I am not a professional chef, this is by no means intended to be a gourmet cookbook, but rather an easy and sometimes unique way of preparing wild game and fish into tasty dishes. For those who do not hunt and/or fish, these recipes can easily be adapted to any meat, fowl, fish, or seafood purchased at the supermarket.

I would like to express a word of advice. Always be extremely careful when handling food. Wash hands thoroughly after handling meat, fish, or fowl, as well as any knives, utensils, cutting boards or counters. Always keep foods well refrigerated and if in doubt — throw it out! I never keep perishable dips for more than one week, even though they are refrigerated, because my recipes do not contain preservatives.

Keeping fish fresh when you are fishing should pose no problem if you always remember to have ice packs or ice handy in a nearby cooler to collect your catch of the day. After cleaning your catch and preparing for freezing, it would be my advice to wrap it tightly in clear plastic wrap, then waxed freezer paper, and don't forget to add the date. Fish can also be frozen by placing in water in a plastic bag or plastic container. This prevents freezer burn and allows the fish to be kept frozen for a longer time.

Listed below are examples of some of the game, fowl, fish, and seafood I have used over the years to prepare my recipes:

<u>Wild Ducks</u>
    Black
    Canvas back
    Green wing teal
    Mallard
    Wood

<u>Domestic Duck</u>
    Muscovy

Geese
    Canadian
    Snow

Game Birds
    Grouse
    Pheasant
    Quail
    Turkey

Small Game
    Rabbit
    Squirrel

Large Game
    Antelope
    Black bear
    Caribou
    Elk
    Moose
    Mule deer
    White tail deer

Fresh Water Fish
  Bluegill   Rock bass
  Catfish   Small mouth bass
  Crappie bass   Walleye
  Large mouth bass   White Perch
  Muskie   Yellow Perch

Salt Water Fish
  Bluefish   Striped bass
  Flounder   Tautog
  Kingfish   Yellow fin tuna
  Sea trout

Shellfish and Crustacean
  Clam   Oyster
  Crab   Scallop
  Mussel   Shrimp

It is my hope that you will try these recipes and see for yourself
that wild game does not have to taste "wild" and that there are
many ways to fix game and fish that will please your palate.
Use your imagination!

FOREWARD (Continued)

Special thanks go to:

- all my friends who kept me well supplied with wild game and fish over the years,

- my wife, Nancy, who tasted and typed,

- my editors, Carolee Kipp and Jane Moyer, for their time, talent, and patience in proofreading and, last, but not least,

- all my tasters who helped to make this cookbook a reality.

Enjoy!

Dale L. Shelly
June, 2000

BARBEQUE

NOTES

DUCK

5 cups chopped duck
2 tablespoons butter or oil
4 cups chopped onions
2 cups grated carrots
4 cups chopped celery
1 tablespoon minced garlic
1/4 teaspoon black pepper
2 tablespoons vinegar
2 tablespoons soy sauce
1 tablespoon chili powder
3/4 cup light brown sugar
4 tablespoons yellow mustard
3 cups ketchup
1/2 cup burgundy or red wine (optional)

In a large skillet, saute' the duck, onions, carrots, celery, and garlic in butter or oil until tender.   Add the remaining ingredients, mixing thoroughly. Simmer 45 to 60 minutes.

SMOKED DUCK

1-1/2 pounds smoked duck, finely chopped
1 cup smoked duck stock or 1 cup ham broth
2 cups chopped celery
1-1/2 cups chopped onions
2 tablespoons parsley flakes
2 tablespoons barbeque sauce, Cajun style
2 tablespoons yellow mustard
2-1/2 cups ketchup
1 tablespoon soy sauce
2 tablespoons sweet pickle relish
4 tablespoons light brown sugar
1 tablespoon vinegar
1 tablespoon chili powder

Combine duck stock, celery, onions, and parsley in a large kettle. Cook until tender. Add chopped duck and the remaining ingredients. Stir. Simmer for 30 minutes, stirring occasionally.

GOOSE

1 pound goose, cooked and chopped
1 cup chopped celery
1 cup chopped onions or leeks
3/4 cup grated carrots
1/2 cup chopped green pepper
1/2 cup mushroom pieces
2 tablespoons parsley flakes
1 teaspoon salt
1/4 teaspoon black pepper
1/2 teaspoon Blackened Redfish Magic®*
1/2 teaspoon Cajun seasoning
3 cups ketchup
2-1/2 tablespoons light brown sugar
2 tablespoons vinegar
2 tablespoons soy sauce
1 cup red wine

Using a large kettle, saute' goose, celery, onions or leeks, carrots, green peppers, and mushrooms in butter or oil until tender. Add the remaining ingredients and simmer approximately 30 minutes.

*Chef Paul Prudhomme's Magic Seasoning Blends®

RABBIT OR SQUIRREL

·5 cups cooked rabbit or squirrel, finely chopped
1 cup chopped celery
1-1/2 cups chopped onions
1 cup grated carrots
1/2 teaspoon oregano
1/4 teaspoon Cajun seasoning
4 tablespoons light brown sugar
4 tablespoons yellow mustard
4 cups ketchup
1 tablespoon soy sauce
1 tablespoon vinegar

·In a pressure cooker, cook four rabbits or eight squirrels in
1-1/2 quarts of water and two teaspoons salt for 45 minutes.
Or, if you prefer, cook in a five quart kettle in two quarts of water
and two teaspoons salt until tender. Cool meat and cut into small
pieces.

Combine all of the above ingredients and mix thoroughly. Bring
to a boil and simmer for 30 minutes.

VENISON

2 pounds ground venison
2 large onions, chopped
2 large carrots, grated
2 large ribs celery, chopped
1 large green or red pepper, chopped
1/2 cup red wine or burgundy
1 tablespoon Worcestershire sauce
1 tablespoon soy sauce
3 cups ketchup
3 tablespoons light brown sugar
3 tablespoons yellow mustard
2 tablespoons vinegar
1/4 cup oatmeal

Combine the first five ingredients in a large skillet. Saute' until tender. Add remaining ingredients, mixing well. Simmer for one hour.

BRINES AND MARINADES

NOTES

BRINE FOR SMOKING FOWL AND GAME BIRDS

5 quarts water
2-1/2 cups Tender Quick® meat cure or
    2-1/2 cups plain (not iodized) salt
3 cups light brown sugar
2 tablespoons meat tenderizer
1 teaspoon Cajun seasoning
1 tablespoon Blackened Redfish Magic®
5 to 7 pounds breast meat, legs, or thighs (skinned and boned)
    livers, hearts, and gizzards

Combine water and spices in a large container. Mix thoroughly. Add breast meat (legs, thighs, hearts, livers, and gizzards can also be cured in the brine). For small fowl, leave in brine 12 hours and for large fowl, leave in brine 18 hours (stir occasionally). Remove from brine, do not rinse. Place meat on smoker racks and set temperature at 140 to 150 degrees. It should take approximately five hours to smoke. After smoking, cook meat in pressure cooker with 1-1/2 quarts water for one hour. If using a regular kettle, add two quarts water and cook until tender. Stock may be saved to make soup.

This brine may be used for large domestic (beef) or wild game (venison, elk, etc.) animals. Marinate in small pieces for thorough penetration. See Page 11 for Dips.

BRINE FOR SMOKING FRESH WATER FISH

5 quarts water

1 cup plain salt (not iodized)

2/3 cup Tender Quick® meat cure
    or 2/3 cup plain (not iodized) salt

2 teaspoons ground black pepper

4 cups light brown sugar

2 tablespoons ground mustard

2 tablespoons garlic powder

2 tablespoons onion powder

2 teaspoons Blackened Redfish Magic®

2 tablespoons soy sauce

6 bay leaves

3 to 5 pounds fresh water fish, skinned and filleted
        or
3 to 5 pounds whole fish, cleaned

Combine all ingredients, reserving fish, in a large container and mix thoroughly. Place fish in brine and marinate in refrigerator for seven hours for small fish fillets or 14 hours for whole fish. Stir occasionally. Remove fish from brine.   DISCARD BRINE. Preheat smoker at approximately 140 to 150 degrees, using flavored wood chips. Place fish on racks in smoker and smoke until fish are tender — do not over smoke.

BRINE FOR SMOKING SALT WATER FISH

5 quarts water

1 cup plain salt   (not iodized)

2/3 cup Tender Quick® meat cure or 2/3 cup plain salt

4 cups light brown sugar

1 tablespoon ground black pepper

1 tablespoon ground mustard

2 tablespoons lemon juice

2 tablespoons garlic powder

2 tablespoons onion powder

2 tablespoons soy sauce

2 tablespoons Worcestershire sauce

1 teaspoon Cajun seasoning

1/2 teaspoon crab and shrimp seasoning

1 teaspoon Blackened Redfish Magic®

8 bay leaves

3 to 5 pounds salt water fish fillets or whole fish

Combine all ingredients, reserving fish, in a large container and mix thoroughly. Place fish in brine and marinate in refrigerator for 8 hours for small fillets; 14 hours for large fillets; and 18 hours for whole fish, stirring occasionally.   Remove fish from brine. DISCARD BRINE. Preheat smoker at approximately 140 to 150 degrees. Place fish on racks in smoker and smoke until meat separates from the bone if using for dip. If smoking to eat as is, smoke harder, if desired.

MARINADES

Some people prefer to marinate wild game before it is cooked to reduce some of the "wild" taste. Here are a few marinades I have used:

1. 2 cups very strong black coffee
    1 cup burgundy or red wine
    2 tablespoons soy sauce
    1 tablespoon Worcestershire sauce

2. 3 quarts water
    2 tablespoons baking soda
    2 tablespoons plain salt (not iodized)
    1 cup vinegar

3. 3 quarts water
    2 tablespoons garlic powder
    2 tablespoons onion powder
    2 tablespoons lemon juice
    1 tablespoon plain salt (not iodized)

Marinate in refrigerator approximately six to eight hours, turning the meat occasionally. Rinse before cooking.

DIPS

NOTES

CRAB

1 pound lump crab meat (thoroughly cleaned)
2 jumbo eggs, hard boiled
3/4 cup minced onions
1/2 teaspoon salt
3/4 teaspoon black pepper
1/2 teaspoon Blackened Redfish Magic®
1/4 teaspoon creole seasoning
3/4 teaspoon crab and shrimp seasoning
1/2 teaspoon paprika
1 tablespoon parsley flakes
4 ounces cream cheese
1-3/4 cups mayonnaise

Grind crab meat and hard boiled eggs using a fine grinding disk. Add the remaining ingredients, combining cream cheese and mayonnaise last. Mix thoroughly. Chill.

Cooked shrimp or scallops may be substituted for the crab.

SMOKED DUCK

1/2 pound smoked duck breast, cooked
3 large eggs, hard boiled
1 small onion, minced
1 teaspoon lemon juice
1/4 teaspoon thyme
1/2 teaspoon ground mustard
1 teaspoon garlic powder
1/4 teaspoon black pepper
1/2 teaspoon paprika
1 tablespoon parsley flakes
4 ounces cream cheese
2-3/4 cups mayonnaise

Grind duck and hard boiled eggs, using a fine grinding disk. Add the remaining ingredients, combining cream cheese and mayonnaise last. Mix thoroughly. Chill.

This dip may be adapted to any domestic (beef) or wild game (venison, elk, etc.) animal.

SMOKED FRESH WATER FISH

1/2 pound smoked fish, skinned and boned
2 extra large eggs, hard boiled
1 small onion, minced
1/2 teaspoon garlic powder
1/4 teaspoon black pepper
1/2 teaspoon ground mustard
3/4 teaspoon paprika
1 tablespoon parsley flakes
2 cups mayonnaise
4 ounces cream cheese

Grind the fish and hard boiled eggs, using a fine grinding disk. Add the remaining ingredients, combining mayonnaise and softened cream cheese last. Mix thoroughly. Chill.

SMOKED SALT WATER FISH DIP

1/2 pound smoked fish, skinned and boned
3 large eggs, hard boiled
1 medium onion, minced
1/2 teaspoon Blackened Redfish Magic®
1/2 teaspoon garlic powder
1/4 teaspoon black pepper
3/4 teaspoon ground mustard
1/2 teaspoon paprika
1/4 teaspoon celery salt
1 tablespoon parsley flakes
1 tablespoon lemon juice
2-3/4 cups mayonnaise
4 ounces cream cheese

Grind the fish and eggs, using a fine grinding disk. Add the next eight ingredients and combine with fish in a large bowl. Add mayonnaise, softened cream cheese, and lemon juice. Mix thoroughly. Chill.

SMOKED GOOSE LIVER PATE'

1/2 pound smoked goose livers, cooked
2 jumbo eggs, hard boiled
1 cup minced onions
1/4 teaspoon Cajun seasoning
1/2 teaspoon ground mustard
1/4 teaspoon black pepper
1/2 teaspoon Blackened Redfish Magic®
1 teaspoon soy sauce
2 teaspoons Worcestershire sauce
1/2 teaspoon paprika
1/2 teaspoon garlic powder
2 tablespoons parsley flakes
4 ounces cream cheese
3/4 to 1 cup mayonnaise

Grind livers and hard boiled eggs, using a fine grinding disk. Add the remaining ingredients, combining the cream cheese and mayonnaise last. Mix thoroughly. Chill.

TURKEY SPREAD

1 pound turkey breast, legs, or thighs, cooked and skinned
5 large eggs, hard boiled
1 medium onion, minced
1 teaspoon soy sauce
1 teaspoon Worcestershire sauce
1-1/2 teaspoons garlic powder
3/4 teaspoon Blackened Redfish Magic®
1 teaspoon ground mustard
1 tablespoon vinegar
1 teaspoon paprika
1/2 teaspoon black pepper
3 to 4 cups mayonnaise
8 ounces cream cheese

Grind the cooked turkey and hard boiled eggs using a fine grinding disk. Add all the other ingredients, combining the mayonnaise and cream cheese last. Mix thoroughly. Chill.

SALADS

NOTES

CRAB

1 - 6 ounce can jumbo lump crab meat, thoroughly cleaned
2 large eggs, hard boiled and chopped
1 small onion, chopped
1/2 teaspoon crab and shrimp seasoning
1/2 teaspoon salt
1/4 teaspoon black pepper
3/4 cup mayonnaise
2 tablespoons sour cream

Combine above ingredients, blending well. Chill.

One-half pound fresh, cleaned shrimp may be substituted for the crab.

DUCK

3 cups cooked duck breast, finely chopped
1 cup chopped celery
1-1/2 cups chopped onions
3 jumbo eggs, hard boiled and chopped
1 tablespoon parsley flakes
1/2 teaspoon salt
1/4 teaspoon black pepper
1/4 teaspoon Blackened Redfish Magic®
1 teaspoon paprika
1 teaspoon ground mustard
3 ounces cream cheese
2 cups mayonnaise

Combine the above ingredients, adding the cream cheese and mayonnaise last. Mix thoroughly. Chill.

PHEASANT

3 cups pheasant breast, cooked and chopped
1 teaspoon salt
1/4 teaspoon black pepper
1/2 teaspoon Blackened Redfish Magic®
1/2 teaspoon paprika
1 cup chopped onions
1 cup chopped celery
3 tablespoons sweet pickle relish
1 tablespoon apple cider vinegar
1-3/4 cups mayonnaise
4 ounces cream cheese
3 jumbo eggs, hard boiled and finely chopped

Combine the above ingredients in a large bowl, adding the mayonnaise and cream cheese last. Mix thoroughly. Chill.

SALMON

1-1/2 pounds salmon
1 quart of water
2 teaspoons salt
1 cup minced onions
3/4 cup finely chopped celery
1/2 cup finely chopped red bell pepper
1/2 teaspoon black pepper
1/2 teaspoon ground red pepper
1/2 teaspoon salt
1 teaspoon Blackened Redfish Magic®
3 tablespoons parsley flakes
4 jumbo eggs, hard boiled and finely chopped
4 ounces cream cheese
2 cups mayonnaise

Place salmon in a large kettle with one quart of water and two teaspoons salt and cook for 30 minutes. Drain, remove skin, and break into small pieces. Set aside to cool. Combine the remaining ingredients in a large mixing bowl, adding cooled salmon, cream cheese, and mayonnaise last. Mix thoroughly. Chill before serving.

SMOKED SALMON

1 pound smoked salmon, finely chopped
1 cup chopped celery
1-1/2 cups chopped onions
3 jumbo eggs, hard boiled and finely chopped
1/4 teaspoon black pepper
1 teaspoon ground mustard
1/2 teaspoon mesquite seasoning
1 teaspoon paprika
2 tablespoons parsley flakes
2 tablespoons sour cream
2 cups mayonnaise

Combine the above ingredients in a large bowl, adding the sour cream and mayonnaise last. Mix thoroughly. Chill.

YELLOW FIN TUNA

1 pound yellow fin tuna
2 cups water
1-1/2 teaspoons salt
3/4 cup diced celery
3/4 cup chopped onions
4 large eggs, hard boiled and chopped
1 tablespoon parsley flakes
1 teaspoon vinegar
1 teaspoon Worcestershire sauce
3/4 teaspoon Old Bay® seasoning
1/4 teaspoon lemon pepper
1/4 teaspoon black pepper
1-1/2 cups mayonnaise
2 tablespoons sour cream

Cook tuna in water and salt until tender. While tuna is cooking, combine all of the above ingredients, adding the mayonnaise and sour cream last. Cool the tuna, cut into small pieces, and add to above mixture. Chill.

SMOKED TURKEY

2 pounds smoked turkey, cooked
2 cups chopped onions
2 cups chopped celery
6 jumbo eggs, hard boiled and chopped
1-1/2 teaspoons black pepper
1 teaspoon salt
1 teaspoon creole seasoning
1/4 teaspoon thyme
1-1/2 teaspoons paprika
2 tablespoons parsley flakes
4 ounces cream cheese
1 cup mayonnaise

Chop smoked turkey and add all of the remaining ingredients in a large bowl. Mix thoroughly. Chill.

SOUPS AND CHOWDERS

NOTES

CRAB

2 pounds lump crab meat, thoroughly cleaned
1 cup chopped onions
3/4 cup chopped celery
3 tablespoons butter
1 teaspoon salt
1/4 teaspoon black pepper
1/2 teaspoon Old Bay® seasoning
1/2 teaspoon crab and shrimp seasoning
1-1/2 cups crushed corn
1 tablespoon parsley
3 jumbo eggs, hard boiled and chopped
1 quart milk
1/2 pint light cream
Cornstarch
Paprika

In a large soup kettle, saute' crab, onions, and celery in butter until tender. Combine remaining ingredients and bring to a boil. Simmer for 30 minutes. To thicken, mix cornstarch with cold water until blended; gradually add to soup. Bring to a boil, stirring constantly until thickened. Sprinkle with paprika before serving.

PHEASANT BURGER

1-1/2 pounds ground pheasant breast
2 tablespoons butter or oil
2 cups chopped onions
1 cup diced carrots
2 cups chopped celery
1 cup frozen peas
1-1/2 teaspoons salt
1/4 teaspoon black pepper
1 tablespoon parsley flakes
2 - 14 ounce cans chicken broth
1 cup rice, lightly cooked

In a large soup kettle, saute' pheasant, onions, carrots, and celery in butter or oil. Add peas, chicken broth, salt, pepper, parsley, and rice. Simmer for 30 minutes.

PHEASANT PASTINA

1 pound pheasant breast
6 cups chicken broth
3 teaspoons granulated chicken bouillon
2 cups water
1 large onion, chopped
1 large carrot, diced
1 dozen brussels sprouts, quartered
1 cup coarsely chopped broccoli
1/4 teaspoon black pepper
1-1/2 teaspoons salt
3/4 teaspoon garlic salt
1 tablespoon parsley
1-1/2 cups pastina, lightly cooked

Chop pheasant and combine with chicken broth, bouillon, and water. Cook until tender. Add the remaining ingredients, reserving the pastina, and cook 15 minutes. Add pastina and simmer for 15 minutes.

PHEASANT VEGETABLE

1 pheasant, approximately 1 to 3 pounds
2 quarts water
1 - 48 ounce can chicken broth
4 teaspoons granulated chicken bouillon
1 teaspoon salt
1/2 teaspoon creole seasoning
1-1/2 cup diced potatoes
1 cup diced carrots
1 cup diced celery
1 cup chopped onions
1 cup cut string beans
1 cup frozen peas

Cook pheasant, chicken bouillon, salt, and water in a kettle. Cook until tender. Bone and chop pheasant. Strain broth. Combine broth, chicken broth and the remaining ingredients in a large kettle and cook until vegetables are tender. Add chopped pheasant and simmer 15 minutes longer.

RABBIT NOODLE

2 rabbits (cleaned)
1 quart water
1 tablespoon salt
1 large onion, diced
2 large carrots, diced
3 large celery ribs, diced
2 packs frozen white corn
4 jumbo eggs, hard boiled and finely chopped
6 to 8 stems saffron
Pepper to taste
2 - 48 ounce cans chicken broth
1 - 16 ounce pack medium noodles, cooked and drained

Place rabbits in water and salt in a pressure cooker for 45 minutes or cook in a five quart kettle until meat falls off the bones. Cool and cut into small pieces. Cook vegetables. Combine chicken broth, vegetables, hard boiled eggs, rabbit, saffron, and cooked noodles in a large soup kettle. Add additional seasonings to taste and simmer for 15 minutes.

SMOKED DUCK BEAN

6 cups smoked duck, skinned, boned, and chopped
4 quarts water) or 4 quarts of
8 tablespoons ham base) ham broth
2 cups chopped celery
2 cups chopped onions
2 cups diced potatoes
1 teaspoon black pepper
1/2 teaspoon Blackened Redfish Magic®
1-1/2 teaspoons chili powder
1 - 28 ounce can diced tomatoes
1 - 15 ounce can tomato sauce
1 - 3 pound can light red kidney beans, drained
1 - 2 pound can white beans, drained
4 medium cans black beans, drained
6 jumbo eggs, hard boiled and chopped
1 tablespoon lemon juice
Flour

Combine all the ingredients in a large kettle. Bring to a boil and simmer for about one hour or until tender. To thicken, mix flour with cold water until blended and gradually add to soup. Bring to boil, stirring constantly until thickened.

SMOKED GOOSE BEAN

4 cups smoked goose, skinned, boned, and chopped
2 pounds mixed beans
4 quarts water   )   or 4 quarts of
8 tablespoons ham base   )   ham broth
1-1/2 cups chopped onions
2 cups chopped celery
1 - 28 ounce can diced tomatoes
1 tablespoon chili powder
3/4 teaspoon black pepper
4 jumbo eggs, hard boiled and chopped
1 tablespoon lemon juice
Cornstarch

Ten to twelve hours before making soup, soak beans in water, changing water several times until water is clear. Drain.

Cook beans, water, ham base, onions, and celery in a large kettle, simmering for at least one hour.   Add remaining ingredients and simmer for 45 minutes. To thicken, mix cornstarch and water until blended and gradually add to soup. Bring to boil, stirring constantly until thickened.

SMOKED TURKEY SOYBEAN

2 smoked turkey legs and thighs, cooked and chopped
4 tablespoons ham stock
3 quarts water
1-1/2 cups diced onions
1 cup diced carrots
1-1/2 cups diced celery
1/4 teaspoon black pepper
1/4 cup diced red pepper
1 - 14.5 ounce can crushed tomatoes
2 large eggs, hard boiled and chopped
1 pound soy beans, cooked
Salt to taste

Combine the above ingredients in a large soup kettle and bring to a boil. Simmer for one hour.

HEARTY TOMATO VENISON

1 pound ground venison
1 medium onion, chopped
2 large ribs celery, chopped
1 tablespoon salt
1/4 teaspoon black pepper
1/3 teaspoon chili powder
1 - 14 ounce can beef broth
1 - 28 ounce can crushed tomatoes
1 cup minute rice
3 tablespoons sour cream

Saute' first three ingredients in skillet until tender, then add remaining ingredients in a five quart kettle and simmer for 30 minutes.

VENISON BURGER

1-1/2 pounds ground venison
1 medium onion, chopped
1 large carrot, chopped
2 large celery ribs, chopped
1 cup frozen or fresh corn
3/4 cup peas
3/4 cup baby lima beans
1 - 15 ounce can tomato sauce
2 - 14 ounce cans beef broth
Flour

Saute' venison and transfer into large stock pot. Add above ingredients and simmer for one hour or until tender. To thicken, mix flour and water until blended and gradually add to soup. Bring to boil, stirring constantly until thickened.

VENISON BURGER VEGETABLE

2 pounds ground venison
2 tablespoons butter
3 large leeks, chopped
1 - 28 ounce can whole tomatoes
1 - 28 ounce can crushed tomatoes
2 - 48 ounce cans beef broth
1 quart water
3 tablespoons beef bouillon
2-1/2 cups coarsely chopped broccoli
2-1/2 cups green peas
3 cups baby lima beans
3 cups cut green beans
2 cups chopped carrots
1 small head cabbage, chopped
1 large turnip, peeled and diced
1 - 6 ounce can sliced mushrooms
Flour

Saute' venison in butter. Transfer to large stock pot. Add all ingredients, stirring thoroughly. Simmer for one hour or until tender. To thicken, mix flour and water until blended and gradually add to soup. Bring to boil, stirring constantly until thickened.

VENISON VEGETABLE

2 pounds venison roast
2 - 48 ounce cans beef broth
2 quarts water
2 teaspoons beef bouillon
1 teaspoon salt
1/3 teaspoon black pepper
small head cabbage, chopped
4 large ribs celery, chopped
2 large onions, chopped
1 pound bag frozen broccoli, chopped
1 pound bag frozen peas
1 pound bag frozen baby lima beans
1 pound bag frozen white sweet corn
1 pound bag frozen string beans
1 - 28 ounce can crushed tomatoes
1 - 14 ounce can tomato sauce
2 packs brown gravy
3/4 cup flour

Cook the first six ingredients in a large kettle until meat is tender. Remove roast and cut into small pieces. Add the vegetables to the broth and bring to boil; meat can be added while cooking. Reduce heat and simmer for 30 minutes. Combine gravy and flour with water and wisk until smooth. Add to soup and simmer 15 minutes.

CLAM CHOWDER

1 dozen large clams, minced
1 cup water
1 teaspoon salt
1/4 teaspoon black pepper
4 cups diced potatoes
1 cup chopped celery
1 cup chopped onions
2 tablespoons parsley flakes
1/4 teaspoon creole seasoning
3 large eggs, hard boiled and chopped

If clams are frozen in shell, they will be easier to open and mince. Save all the broth from the clams and add to chowder. Combine the ingredients in a large kettle and cook until tender.

Then add:
    1 quart milk
    1/2 pint light cream
    2 tablespoons butter.

Simmer for 15 minute and serve hot.

CLAM CORN CHOWDER

3 dozen medium size clams, minced
2 cups water
5 medium potatoes, diced
3 large ribs celery, chopped
2 large onions, chopped
2 cups white sweet corn
1-1/2 teaspoons salt
1/4 teaspoon black pepper
1 quart milk
3 tablespoons butter
Cornstarch

In a large kettle, cook the clams, water, and clam broth from clams until clams are tender. In a separate kettle, cook the vegetables, salt, and pepper until vegetables are tender. Combine and add milk and butter, cooking until hot, but not boiling. To thicken, mix cornstarch and water until blended and gradually add to soup. Bring to boil, stirring constantly until thickened.

FRESH WATER TROUT CHOWDER

2 pounds trout, cleaned, cooked, and chopped
3 cups water
1 teaspoon salt
2 cups chopped celery
1 cup chopped onions
3 cups diced potatoes
1/4 teaspoon Blackened Redfish Magic®
4 large eggs, hard boiled and chopped
5 cups milk
1 pint light cream
2 tablespoons butter

Combine the water, vegetables, and seasonings and cook until tender. Add the trout, hard boiled eggs, milk, cream, and butter and simmer for 20 minutes.

SMOKED RAINBOW TROUT CHOWDER

3 cups chopped celery
2 cups minced onions
2 cups diced potatoes
2 cups crushed corn
1 teaspoon salt
1/2 teaspoon black pepper
3 tablespoons parsley flakes
1 teaspoon Blackened Redfish Magic®
1/2 teaspoon crab and shrimp seasoning
2 cups water
5 cups smoked trout, finely chopped
1 pint light cream
2 cups milk
4 tablespoons butter
Cornstarch

In a large soup kettle, cook celery, onions, potatoes, corn, salt, pepper and seasonings in two cups water. Cook until vegetables are tender. Add smoked trout, cream, milk, and butter. To thicken, mix cornstarch and water until blended and gradually add to chowder. Bring to boil, stirring constantly until thickened. Simmer 15 minutes.

OYSTER CHOWDER

4 dozen medium size oysters and broth
1-1/2 teaspoons salt
1/8 teaspoon black pepper
1-1/2 cups water
1/2 teaspoon Blackened Redfish Magic®
4 potatoes, peeled and diced
2 celery ribs, chopped
1 medium onion, chopped
3 large eggs, hard boiled and chopped
1 quart milk
1/2 pint light cream
2 tablespoons butter
Paprika

Cook oysters in broth, water, salt, pepper, and Blackened Redfish Magic® for about five minutes. In a separate kettle, cook the potatoes, celery, and onions until tender. Combine the oysters and vegetables with eggs, milk, cream, and butter and simmer until hot, but not boiling. Sprinkle with paprika. Serve hot.

PINK SALMON CHOWDER

8 strips bacon
2 pounds pink salmon (if fresh, skinned and boned)
3 cups water
1 tablespoon salt
4 medium potatoes, diced
3 large ribs celery, diced
1 large onion, diced
3 tablespoons parsley flakes
1/2 teaspoon seafood seasoning
5 large eggs, hard boiled and finely chopped
1 teaspoon liquid smoke (optional)
1 tablespoon soy sauce
2 quarts milk
1 pint light cream
3 tablespoons butter
Flour

Fry bacon until crisp. Remove bacon to paper towel to absorb excess grease. Add salmon to bacon drippings and saute'. In a five quart kettle, add the water, salt, potatoes, celery, onions, parsley flakes, and seafood seasoning. Cook until vegetables are tender and then add eggs, crumbled bacon, salmon, liquid smoke, and soy sauce. Bring to boil. Add milk, cream, and butter. Allow to simmer for about 15 to 20 minutes. To thicken, mix flour and water until blended and gradually add to chowder. Bring to boil, stirring constantly until thickened.

40

SEAFOOD CHOWDER

1 pound haddock, skinned and boned
1/2 pound small shrimp
1/2 pound scallops, cut in half
4 tablespoons butter
1 cup chopped onions
1 cup chopped celery
2 cups diced potatoes
1 cup white corn
1 teaspoon salt
1/4 teaspoon black pepper
2 teaspoons creole seasoning
1-1/2 teaspoons crab and shrimp seasoning
1/4 teaspoon Cajun seasoning
2 cups water
1 - 28 ounce can diced tomatoes
1 - 14 ounce can tomato sauce
1 quart milk
1/2 pint light cream

Saute' the haddock, shrimp, and scallops in 2 tablespoons butter, breaking up the haddock as it is browning. Cook the next 12 ingredients until vegetables are tender. Combine the seafood and vegetables and simmer for 10 minutes. Add the milk, cream, and remaining 2 tablespoons butter and simmer for 5 minutes.

DUCK CORN CHOWDER

3 cups duck breast, skinned
3 tablespoons butter
2 cups water
1 cup chopped onions
1 cup diced carrots
1 cup chopped celery
2 cups diced potatoes
1 - 14 ounce bag frozen white corn, crushed
3 tablespoons parsley flakes
3 teaspoons salt
1 teaspoon black pepper
4 jumbo eggs, hard boiled and chopped
2 cups milk
1/2 cup light cream

Saute' duck breast in two tablespoons butter. Chop and set aside. In a large kettle, combine onions, carrots, celery, potatoes, corn, parsley, salt, and pepper in water and cook until tender. Add duck, hard boiled eggs, milk, cream, and one tablespoon butter. Simmer for 30 minutes.

SMOKED DUCK CHOWDER

3 cups smoked duck, cooked and finely chopped
5 cups smoked duck stock
2 cups chopped celery
2 cups chopped onions
4 cups diced potatoes
1 teaspoon salt
1/4 teaspoon black pepper
3 tablespoons parsley flakes
5 jumbo eggs, hard boiled and chopped
1/2 pint light cream
3 tablespoons butter
Paprika

In a large soup kettle, combine all of the ingredients, reserving the cream, butter and paprika.   Bring to a boil and simmer for 30 minutes. Add the cream and butter and simmer an additional 15 minutes.   Sprinkle with paprika.

STEWS

NOTES

DUCK

4 cups duck breast, uncooked and cut in 1" cubes
2 tablespoons butter or oil
1 - 48 ounce can chicken broth
2 packs onion soup
4 cups diced potatoes
2 cups diced turnips
1 cup diced carrots
2 cups diced celery
1-1/2 cups frozen peas
2 teaspoons salt
1/4 teaspoon black pepper
3/4 cup white wine
Flour

Saute' the duck cubes in butter or oil until tender. Combine the remaining ingredients in a large soup kettle and cook until the vegetables are tender. Add the duck cubes and wine last. To thicken, mix flour and water until well blended and gradually add to stew. Bring to boil, stirring constantly until thickened.

OYSTER

Cook together in a three quart kettle:

4 dozen medium size oysters and broth
1-1/2 teaspoons salt   (more may be desired to taste)
1/4 teaspoon pepper
1/8 teaspoon Blackened Redfish Magic®
1 tablespoon parsley flakes

Heat separately:

2 cups milk
1/2 pint light cream
2 tablespoons butter

When the oysters are cooked, slowly add milk, cream, and butter.
Simmer 5 to 10 minutes and sprinkle with paprika.

RABBIT

4 cups cooked rabbit, cut in pieces
2 - 48 ounce cans beef broth
4 cups chopped celery
3 cups diced carrots
3 cups chopped onions
5 cups diced potatoes
2 cups frozen peas
3 tablespoons parsley flakes
Flour

In a large kettle, combine beef broth, vegetables, and seasonings.
Cook until tender and then add the chopped rabbit.   To thicken,
mix flour and water until well blended and gradually add to stew.
Bring to boil, stirring constantly until thickened.

SQUIRREL

5 squirrels
2 quarts water
3 teaspoons salt
2 cups chopped onions
2 cups chopped celery
2 cups diced carrots
4 cups diced potatoes
2-1/2 cups squirrel stock
1-1/2 teaspoons Blackened Redfish Magic®
2 tablespoons parsley flakes
3 - 10-3/4 ounce cans broccoli cheese soup
Flour

In a pressure cooker, place squirrels in two quarts water and add one teaspoon salt. Cook for at least 45 minutes or until squirrels are tender. Or, you can use a five quart kettle and cook squirrels several hours until tender. Cut into small pieces and set aside.

Combine vegetables, squirrel stock, and seasonings and cook for 20 minutes. Add the broccoli cheese soup and the chopped squirrel. To thicken, mix flour and water until well blended and gradually add to stew. Bring to boil, stirring constantly until thickened. Season to taste.

SMOKED VENISON SAUSAGE

2 pounds venison sausage, sliced 1/2" thick
3 cups water
1 teaspoon salt
1/8 teaspoon black pepper
1 tablespoon parsley flakes
1 large leek or large onion, chopped
2 cups diced potatoes
1 cup chopped celery
1 large carrot, cut in slices
2 cups diced turnips
Flour

Place sausage and water in a five quart kettle and boil 15 minutes. Add the remaining ingredients and cook for 30 minutes or until vegetables are tender. To thicken, mix flour and water until well blended and gradually add to stew. Bring to boil, stirring constantly until thickened.

CROCK POT VENISON

1-1/2 pounds venison steak, cut in 1" cubes
1 - 48 ounce can beef broth
1 pack dry onion soup
3 packs brown gravy
1 medium onion, sliced
2 medium carrots, sliced
2 large ribs celery, sliced
3 large potatoes, cubed
1 - 4 ounce can chopped mushrooms and liquid
1 small green or red pepper, chopped   (optional)
1/2 teaspoon black pepper
1/8 teaspoon ground red pepper
3/4 teaspoon crushed garlic
3/4 cup red wine or burgundy

Combine all ingredients in a crock pot and mix thoroughly. Cook on high for six hours and on low for two or three hours until meat and vegetables are tender.

VENISON

2 pounds steak, cut in 2" cubes
1 cup sliced onions
2 cups chopped celery
2 cups diced carrots
4 cups diced potatoes
1 cup diced sweet potatoes
1/2 teaspoon creole seasoning
1 teaspoon salt
1/4 teaspoon black pepper
1 - 48 ounce can beef broth
3 tablespoons brown gravy mix
Flour

Brown steak cubes in a large soup kettle, then add all ingredients and bring to a rolling boil. Simmer for about one hour or until vegetables are tender. To thicken, mix flour and water until well blended and gradually add to stew. Bring to boil, stirring constantly until thickened

CASSEROLES

NOTES

SMOKED GOOSE AND SCALLOPED POTATOES

2 cups smoked goose, chopped
3 cups sliced potatoes
1 large onion, sliced
1/4 teaspoon thyme
1/4 teaspoon dill seasoning
1/4 teaspoon black pepper
1/2 teaspoon salt
2 tablespoons parsley flakes
1 cup shredded sharp cheese

White sauce:
    3 tablespoons butter
    3 tablespoons flour
    3 cups milk

Melt butter in a 4 quart sauce pan and stir in flour to make a paste. Gradually add milk, stirring constantly, until boiling and thickened. Add salt, pepper, onion, dill, parsley, thyme, and cheese. Simmer until cheese is melted and sauce is smooth. Set aside. Place sliced potatoes and smoked goose in a greased casserole dish and cover with cheese sauce. Sprinkle with paprika. Bake uncovered at 350 degrees for approximately one hour or until browned and bubbling.

GOOSE NOODLE

2 cups goose breasts or thighs, cooked and chopped
1 tablespoon chicken bouillon granules
1 - 14 ounce can chicken broth
2-1/2 cups goose stock
2 cans broccoli cheese soup
1 can cream of celery soup
1 - 4 ounce can mushroom pieces
1 pack dry onion soup
4 or 5 slices bread, buttered and cubed
1 - 12 ounce pack medium noodles

Saute' chopped goose in butter or oil, add chicken broth, bouillon, goose stock, dry onion soup, the creamed soups, and mushroom pieces. Cook noodles for one minute. Drain and put in a deep casserole dish. Pour goose mixture over noodles and mix thoroughly. Top with cubed bread. Bake uncovered at 350 degrees for one hour.

GOOSE AND NOODLE

1-1/2 pounds goose breast, skinned and cut in small pieces
2 tablespoons butter or olive oil
1 - 14 ounce can chicken broth
1/2 cup red wine (optional)
1 pack dry onion soup
2 cans cream of mushroom soup
1 can cream of celery soup
2 tablespoons mayonnaise
2 tablespoons cream cheese
4 or 5 slices bread, buttered and cubed
8 ounce pack medium noodles

Saute' goose in butter or olive oil, add wine, dry onion soup, the creamed soups, mayonnaise, and cream cheese. Cook noodles for one minute. Drain and put in a deep greased casserole dish. Pour goose mixture over noodles and top with cubed bread. Bake uncovered at 350 degrees for 45 to 60 minutes.

BLUEGILL CREOLE

1 - 28 ounce can crushed Italian tomatoes with herbs
1 cup diced onions
1 cup chopped celery
1/4 teaspoon Blackened Redfish Magic®
1-1/2 pounds bluegills, filleted and skinned
3/4 cup Parmesan cheese

Combine the tomatoes, onion, celery, and seasoning in a glass baking dish.   Add fish, stir lightly to combine and sprinkle with Parmesan cheese. Place in oven on middle rack and bake at 350 degrees for 60 minutes. Serve over cooked rice.

SHRIMP AND NOODLE

1-1/2 pounds large shrimp, cleaned and peeled
3/4 cup chopped onion
2 tablespoons butter or olive oil
1 teaspoon salt
1/4 teaspoon black pepper
1/2 teaspoon Old Bay® seasoning
1/4 teaspoon crab and shrimp seasoning
1 tablespoon Worcestershire sauce
1 - 8 ounce pack noodles, cooked
4 pieces of bread, buttered and cubed
3 tablespoons butter
3 tablespoons flour
1-1/4 cups milk

Saute' shrimp and onions in butter and oil until tender. Add the remaining seasonings. In a sauce pan, melt three tablespoons butter and stir in flour; add milk and stir constantly until thickened. Combine with shrimp and onions. Pour mixture over noodles and stir together. Turn into a greased casserole dish and top with buttered bread cubes. Bake at 350 degrees for 45 minutes or until bread cubes are golden brown.

CRAB AND CRAPPIE BASS

1 pound crappie bass fillets, cut in large pieces
1 pound can back fin lump crab meat, thoroughly cleaned
1 - 28 ounce can diced tomatoes
1 - 15 ounce can tomato sauce
1 - 8 ounce can mushroom pieces
1 tablespoon ground mustard
1/2 teaspoon Blackened Redfish Magic®
1/2 teaspoon crab and shrimp seasoning
1/2 teaspoon Cajun seasoning
1/2 teaspoon black pepper
1/4 teaspoon thyme
1 tablespoon parsley flakes
12 ounces mozzarella shredded cheese
Paprika

Combine all of the above ingredients in a large bowl, reserving 6 ounces of the cheese. Mix thoroughly and place in a large greased casserole. Top with the reserved cheese and sprinkle with paprika. Bake covered for one hour at 350 degrees and 15 minutes uncovered.

CRAPPIE BASS AND PASTA

12 crappie bass, filleted
Flour
3 tablespoons olive oil
1 teaspoon minced garlic
1/3 cup white raisins
1 teaspoon salt
1/4 teaspoon Cajun seasoning
1/4 teaspoon creole seasoning
6 stems saffron
1-1/2 cups penne pasta, cooked
Parmesan cheese

Dredge the crappie bass in flour and pan fry in oil until browned on both sides. Drain and set aside. Combine the pasta, garlic, raisins, salt, seasonings, and saffron. In a large greased casserole dish, place a layer of crappies and cover with the pasta mixture. Continue layering and top with Parmesan cheese. Bake, covered, at 350 degrees for 30 minutes

DUCK NOODLE

1 pound duck breast, boned, skinned, and cubed
2 tablespoons butter or olive oil
1/4 teaspoon salt
1/4 teaspoon black pepper
1/4 cup diced leeks or onions
1/4 cup diced green pepper
3/4 cup mushroom pieces
2 packs dry chicken gravy
2 cups water
1/4 cup white wine   (optional)
1/2 pint light cream
1- 8 ounce pack medium noodles
Cheddar cheese crackers, crushed

Saute' the duck in butter or oil together with salt, pepper, onions, green peppers, and mushrooms.   Add gravy and water and stir until thickened. Add the remaining ingredients to the skillet and mix thoroughly. Cook noodles for two minutes.

Place the noodles in a greased casserole dish and pour the duck mixture over the noodles, stirring together. Top with crackers and bake uncovered at 350 degrees for one hour or until brown around the edges.

SMOKED GOOSE NOODLE

4 cups smoked goose, chopped
6 tablespoons butter
6 tablespoons flour
2 cups milk
1/2 teaspoon salt
1/2 teaspoon black pepper
1/2 teaspoon Blackened Redfish Magic®
1 tablespoon soy sauce
1 can cream of mushroom soup
1 can cream of celery soup
1 cup frozen peas
1 - 4 ounce can mushroom pieces
Bread crumbs
Paprika
1 - 12 ounce pack medium noodles, lightly cooked

In a sauce pan, prepare a white sauce as follows: Melt butter, stir in flour to form a paste, gradually add milk, stirring constantly until thick and boiling. To the white sauce, stir in the cream of mushroom soup and cream of celery soup. Add the remaining ingredients, reserving the bread crumbs and paprika. Pour into a large greased casserole dish and top with bread crumbs and paprika. Bake at 350 degrees for one hour.

SMOKED GOOSE

3 cups smoked goose, chopped
3 tablespoons butter
3 tablespoons flour
2 cups milk
1 teaspoon salt
1/4 teaspoon black pepper
1 tablespoon granulated ham stock
1 teaspoon thyme
1 tablespoon Worcestershire sauce
1 can cream of chicken soup
1 can cream of broccoli soup
1 - 6 ounce can mushroom pieces
2 cups cut string beans
Cracker crumbs

In a three quart sauce pan, make a white sauce as follows: Melt butter, stir in flour to make a paste, gradually add milk, stirring constantly until thick and boiling. To the white sauce, add the cream of chicken soup and cream of broccoli soup. Add the remaining ingredients, reserving the cracker crumbs, and mix thoroughly. Pour into a large, greased casserole dish and top with cracker crumbs. Bake at 350 degrees for one hour or until bubbling and crumbs are browned.

SMOKED PHEASANT

4 tablespoons butter
4 tablespoons flour
2 cups milk
1/2 teaspoon salt
1/4 teaspoon black pepper
1 large onion, chopped
1 tablespoon parsley flakes
5 medium potatoes sliced
2 cups smoked pheasant, cooked and coarsely chopped
1 cup shredded sharp cheese
Paprika

In a large sauce pan make a white sauce using butter, flour, milk, salt, and pepper. To boiling white sauce, add onion, parsley flakes, and pheasant and stir together. Remove from heat. Place half the mixture in a large greased casserole dish and cover with sliced potatoes. Cover with remaining mixture. Top with cheese and sprinkle paprika over cheese. Bake at 350 degrees for 45 minutes or until bubbling and brown around the edges.

PHEASANT AND SALSA

4 cups pheasant breast, cut in 2" cubes
1 cup chopped green pepper
2 cups chopped onion
1 teaspoon crushed garlic
2 teaspoons salt
1/4 teaspoon black pepper
1 - 12 ounce can diced tomatoes
1 - 16 ounce jar mild or medium salsa
1 - 4 ounce can mushroom pieces (including mushroom broth)
2 tablespoons butter
1 tablespoon olive oil
3 tablespoons sour cream
8 ounces sharp cheddar cheese
1 - 12 ounce pack medium noodles, cooked
6 slices of bread, buttered and cubed

Saute' the pheasant, onions, green pepper, garlic, salt, and pepper in butter and olive oil until tender. In a large bowl, combine tomatoes, salsa, sour cream, mushrooms, and cheddar cheese. Stir the pheasant mixture and the noodles into the tomato mixture. Turn into a large greased casserole dish and top with bread cubes. Bake uncovered at 350 degrees for 30 minutes, and an additional 30 minutes at 300 degrees.

"PIG STOMACH"

1 pound ground venison
1 pound lean ground pork
4 large potatoes, diced
2 large celery ribs, diced
1 large onion, diced
1 large carrot, diced
2 large eggs
1 small green pepper, diced   (optional)
2 tablespoons parsley flakes
2 teaspoons salt
1/2 teaspoon black pepper

Combine all the above ingredients in a large bowl and mix thoroughly. Place in a deep buttered casserole dish.   Bake, covered, at 350 degrees for one to one and a half hours, and uncovered for 30 minutes until browned.

This can also be stuffed in a large, CLEANED, pig stomach. Place in a roasting pan with two cups water. Bake at 350 degrees for approximately three hours.

VENISON TOMATO AND CHEESE

1 pound ground venison
1 large onion, chopped
2 ribs celery, chopped
1 medium green pepper, chopped (optional)
1 - 28 ounce can crushed tomatoes
1 - 15 ounce can tomato sauce
1/4 cup salsa (mild or medium)
1 teaspoon salt
1/4 teaspoon black pepper
2-1/4 cups macaroni, cooked
8 ounces shredded white sharp cheddar cheese

Saute' the ground venison, onion, celery, and pepper in a large skillet. Add the tomatoes, tomato sauce, salsa, salt, pepper, and macaroni. Mix thoroughly. Place in a greased casserole dish and cover with cheese. Bake, covered, at 350 degrees for 45 minutes. Uncover for last few minutes to brown cheese.

VENISON BURGER AND POTATO

1 pound ground venison
1 large onion, chopped
2 cups green beans
2 cups diced potatoes
1/4 cup green peas
1 can cream of mushroom soup
1 can cream of celery soup
1/4 cup light cream
1/4 teaspoon salt
1/4 teaspoon black pepper

Brown venison and onion in a large skillet. Add the beans, peas, potatoes, soups, salt, pepper, and light cream. Mix thoroughly. Transfer to a large, greased baking dish. Bake at 350 degrees uncovered for one hour or until browned and bubbling.

VENISON BURGER MACARONI AND CHEESE

1/2 pound ground venison
1/2 pound lean ground beef
1 large onion, chopped
1 large carrot, chopped
1 tablespoon crushed garlic
2 tablespoons butter or vegetable oil
1 teaspoon salt
1/4 teaspoon black pepper
3 packs brown gravy mix
3 cups water
2 cups frozen peas
8 ounces shredded sharp cheddar cheese
2 cups macaroni, cooked

Saute' the first five ingredients in a large skillet using butter or vegetable oil. Add seasonings. Mix gravy and water in a sauce pan as directed and add to the ingredients in the skillet. Bring to a boil for one minute. Add peas and cheese and mix thoroughly. Add macaroni and stir together. Transfer to a large, greased baking dish and bake for 30 minutes or until bubbling.

VENISON AND MACARONI

1-1/2 pounds ground venison
1 large onion, minced
1/4 cup minced green pepper
1 tablespoon butter
1 pack dry onion soup
2 cans mushroom soup
2 cans celery soup
1 cup shredded sharp cheddar cheese
2 cups macaroni, cooked
1 cup cracker crumbs

Combine the first four ingredients in a large skillet. Saute' until tender. Add the remaining ingredients, reserving the cracker crumbs, and mix thoroughly. Transfer to a large greased casserole dish and top with cracker crumbs. Bake uncovered at 350 degrees 30 to 45 minutes.

VENISON SHORT RIBS

2 or 3 pounds short ribs
2 cups water
1 cup diced carrots
2 cups chopped onions
2 cups chopped red bell peppers
2 cups chopped celery
1 teaspoon minced garlic
2 cups diced eggplant
1 teaspoon salt
1 teaspoon black pepper
3 tablespoons barbeque sauce
2 tablespoons Worcestershire sauce
1 tablespoon soy sauce
1 - 28 ounce can diced tomatoes
1 - 6 ounce can tomato paste
2 tablespoons hot sauce   (optional)

In a five quart kettle, brown short ribs; then add water, salt, and pepper and simmer for about two hours. In another large kettle, add the remaining ingredients and bring to a boil, cooking for 15 minutes. Remove the rib bones and place short ribs in a deep casserole dish. Pour vegetables over the meat and bake uncovered at 350 degrees for one hour. Serve over cooked pasta.

VENISON

1/2 pound ground venison
1/2 pound ground sirloin
1 medium onion, minced
1/2 cup barbeque sauce
1 teaspoon vinegar
2 tablespoons brown sugar
1 teaspoon chili powder
1/2 cup shredded sharp cheddar cheese
1 - 8 ounce pack medium noodles, cooked one minute
Crushed crackers

Brown the venison, sirloin, and onions in a skillet. Combine all the ingredients in a large casserole dish. Sprinkle crushed crackers over the top. Bake uncovered at 350 degrees for 45 minutes.

VENISON STEAK

1 pound venison steak, cut in 1" cubes
1 medium onion, diced
1 small green pepper, diced
2 tablespoons butter or oil
1 can cream of mushroom soup
1 can celery soup
1 can onion soup
1/4 teaspoon black pepper
8 ounce pack medium noodles, cooked
4 slices bread, buttered and cubed

Saute' the steak, onion, and pepper in a large skillet using butter or oil until tender. Add the remaining ingredients. Mix thoroughly and simmer. Place noodles in a deep casserole dish and pour venison mixture over noodles. Cover with bread cubes. Bake uncovered at 350 degrees for 45 minutes to one hour.

PIES AND POT PIES

NOTES

STELLA'S PIE CRUST

2 cups flour
2/3 cup shortening
1 teaspoon salt
4 tablespoons water

Using a pastry blender, or with your hands, combine flour, shortening, and salt. Blend together until you have coarse crumbs, then add one tablespoon of water at a time, tossing with a fork until all water has been added. Form into ball, divide in half, and, using a rolling pin, roll between waxed paper to desired size.

This recipe is for two nine inch pie crusts.

PIE CRUST

	1X	2X	3X	4X
Flour	1-1/3 cups	2-2/3	4	5-1/3
Shortening	1/2 cup	1	1-1/2	2
Salt	1/2 teaspoon	1	1-1/2	2
Cold water	3 teaspoons	6	9	12

Using pastry blender (or with your hands) combine flour, shortening, and salt. Blend together until you have coarse crumbs, then add one tablespoon of water at a time, tossing with a fork until all water has been added. Knead into a large ball. Separate into as many sections as pie shells you are making and, using rolling pin, roll between waxed paper to desired size.

Pastry shell - bake at 425 degrees for about 15 minutes or until browned.

Bake all pies on the bottom oven rack.

DUCK

4 cups chopped duck breast
2 tablespoons butter
1/4 cup diced mushrooms
I cup chopped celery
2 cups chopped onions
I cup chopped carrots
I cup frozen peas
I tablespoon parsley flakes
I teaspoon salt
1/4 teaspoon black pepper
I tablespoon soy sauce
Pinch of saffron
2 packs beef gravy
4 cups water
2 - 9" unbaked pie crusts

Saute' duck breast in butter until tender. Add all of the above ingredients, reserving the beef gravy and 2 cups water. Simmer until vegetables are tender. Combine the duck and vegetables and prepare gravy using the remaining two cups of water. To thicken, mix flour and water until well blended and gradually add to mixture. Bring to boil, stirring constantly until thickened. Pour into a pastry lined pie dish and cover with top crust. Bake on lower rack in oven at 425 degrees for 15 minutes, then 350 degrees for 45 or 50 minutes or until crust is lightly browned.

73

OYSTER

3 dozen oysters and broth

1 cup diced potatoes	) Cook in oyster broth and
1 small onion, diced	) about 1/3 to 1/2 cup water
1 rib celery, diced	) until tender. Thicken with
2 teaspoons salt	) flour if desired. Season to
1/8 teaspoon black pepper	) taste.
Flour	)

2 - 10" unbaked pie crusts

Butter the inside of the bottom unbaked pie crust. Mix raw oysters together with cooked vegetables. Pour mixture into pie shell, add small amount of milk, leaving about one inch from top of crust. Cover with top crust and bake on the bottom oven rack at 425 degrees for about 20 minutes and then 375 degrees for at least 40 minutes or until crust is browned and inside mixture is bubbling.

PHEASANT

2 cups chopped pheasant
1 pack onion soup
1 cup water
2 cups chicken broth
1-1/2 cups frozen peas
1 cup chopped celery
2 cups chopped onions
1/2 cup chopped carrots
2 cups diced potatoes
2 tablespoons parsley flakes
1 teaspoon salt
1/4 teaspoon black pepper
Flour
2 - 9" unbaked pie crusts

Combine all of the ingredients in a large kettle. Cook until vegetables are tender. To thicken, mix flour and water until well blended and gradually add to broth. Bring to boil, stirring constantly until thickened. Place in a pastry lined pie dish and cover with top crust. Bake on lower oven rack at 425 degrees for 15 minutes, then 350 degrees for 45 minutes or until crust is lightly browned.

RABBIT

2 whole rabbits
1 quart water
1 tablespoon salt
2 cups chopped celery
1 cup chopped onion
1-1/2 cups diced carrots
3 cups diced potatoes
1/4 cup chopped red bell pepper
1 teaspoon black pepper
1 teaspoon Blackened Redfish Magic®
2 tablespoons parsley flakes
4 cups chicken broth
Flour
2 - 9" unbaked pie crusts

Using a kettle or pressure cooker, cook rabbits in one quart water and one tablespoon salt until tender. Cut into small pieces and set aside. Cook remaining ingredients until tender, salt to taste. Combine the rabbits with the vegetables and thicken as desired.

Prepare pie crust and cover bottom of pie dish. Spoon mixture into pie shell and cover with top crust. Bake on bottom rack of oven at 425 degrees for 20 minutes, reduce heat to 350 degrees for 45 minutes or until crust is lightly browned.

VENISON

1 pound venison steak, cut into small pieces
2 tablespoons butter
1-1/2 cups minced onions
1-1/2 cups diced celery
2 cups diced potatoes
1 cup sliced carrots
1 tablespoon parsley flakes
6 stems saffron
2 packs brown gravy
2 cups water
1 small can beef broth
Flour
2 - 9" unbaked pie crusts

Saute' steak, butter, onions, and celery in a skillet until tender. Combine two packs of brown gravy, two cups of water, and beef broth and heat to boiling, stirring constantly. Add to skillet, together with potatoes, carrots, parsley, and saffron. Simmer for about 15 minutes. Thicken with flour. Pour into a 9" prepared unbaked pie shell and cover with pie crust. Bake at 425 degrees for 15 minutes, then reduce to 350 degrees and continue baking for 45 minutes or until crust is lightly browned.

STELLA'S POT PIE DOUGH

1 large egg
3/4 cup milk
2-1/3 cups all purpose flour

Beat egg vigorously in a large bowl. Add milk. Gradually mix in flour a little at a time with a fork until flour stiffens. Using the fork, take a small amount of dough and place on a pie board. Sprinkle flour on the board and on the rolling pin; add flour to the dough as needed when rolling out. Roll very thin and cut into small squares (a pizza cutter is good for this). Using a thin spatula, remove from board and drop each piece in boiling broth one at a time so they do not clump together. Simmer for 15 minutes or until pot pie dough is soft.

DUCK POT PIE

1 - 48 ounce can chicken broth
2 - 14 ounce cans chicken broth
1 teaspoon salt
1 cup chopped onions
1 cup chopped celery
2-1/2 cups diced potatoes
1/4 teaspoon black pepper
1 teaspoon garlic powder
2 tablespoons parsley flakes
Pinch of saffron
2 packs chicken gravy
2 cups duck, cooked and chopped
Pot pie dough

In a large soup kettle, combine chicken broth, vegetables, and seasonings, and bring to a boil. Stir in gravy and add duck. Prepare pot pie dough — refer to pot pie dough recipe.

SMOKED GOOSE POT PIE

2 cups goose legs, thighs, or breasts, cooked and chopped
1 gallon smoked goose stock
2 cups diced potatoes
1 cup chopped celery
1 cup chopped onions
1 tablespoon parsley
Pinch of saffron   (optional)
Salt and pepper to taste
Pot pie dough

Combine goose stock, vegetables, saffron, salt, and pepper in a large kettle. Cook until tender; add chopped goose . Prepare pot pie dough — refer to pot pie dough recipe.

VENISON POT PIE

2 pounds venison roast
2 - 48 ounce cans beef broth
2 cups water
1 teaspoon salt
1/4 teaspoon black pepper
1 large onion, chopped
Pinch of saffron
4 cups diced potatoes
3 large ribs celery, chopped
1 tablespoon parsley
Pot pie dough

Cook venison in beef broth, water, salt, pepper, onion, and saffron until tender (approximately 2 hours). Remove meat from broth and cut in small pieces. Add the potatoes, celery, and parsley to broth and cook until tender. Add meat and simmer. Prepare pot pie dough — refer to pot pie dough recipe.

FOWL

NOTES

DUCK BREAST PATTIES

1 pound duck breasts, cooked and skinned
2 jumbo eggs, hard boiled
3/4 cup mushrooms, finely chopped
1 onion, chopped
1/4 cup minced green pepper
1 teaspoon salt
3/4 teaspoon ground mustard
1 teaspoon lemon juice
2 large eggs
3/4 cup mayonnaise
1 cup bread crumbs

Grind duck breasts and hard boiled eggs using a fine grinding disk. Add mushrooms, onions, green peppers, salt, mustard, lemon juice, eggs, mayonnaise, and bread crumbs. Mix together and form patties. Pan or deep fry.

DUCK AND RICE IN CROCK POT

4 cups duck breast, cut in 2" cubes
2 cans cream of chicken soup
1 can cream of celery soup
2 cups chicken broth
1 cup burgundy or red wine
1 pack onion soup mix
1 teaspoon minced garlic
1 teaspoon onion powder
1 tablespoon parsley flakes
Saffron to taste   (optional)
1-1/4 cups rice

Add all the ingredients in a large crock pot, reserving the rice.
Mix thoroughly and cook on high for six hours, and on low for one
hour.   Add rice and cook for an additional 45 minutes.

DUCK GRAVY AND WAFFLES

3 cups duck breast, cooked and chopped
4 packs chicken gravy
1 pack onion soup
4 cups water
1 cup white wine
6 ounce can sliced mushrooms
1 teaspoon minced garlic
1 tablespoon parsley flakes

Combine the chicken gravy, onion soup, and water. Bring to a
boil, stirring constantly. Add the white wine, mushrooms, garlic,
parsley flakes, and duck. Simmer for ten minutes. Thicken with
flour if desired. Serve over waffles.

FRIED DUCK TENDERS

1 pound duck breasts, sliced in 1" strips
4 large eggs, beaten
Cheddar cheese crackers, finely crushed
Salt and pepper to taste
Butter and olive oil

Dip duck strips in eggs and then cracker crumbs. Pan fry in butter and olive oil until browned on both sides.

CANADIAN GOOSE IN GARLIC SAUCE

2 pounds goose breast, skinned, boned, and julienned
4 cups chicken stock
1 tablespoon white vinegar
2 tablespoons soy sauce
2 tablespoons chicken bouillon
3 tablespoons brown sugar
1/4 teaspoon ground ginger
2 tablespoons minced garlic
1/4 teaspoon salt
1/4 teaspoon black pepper
3 tablespoons butter
1 large leek, julienned
2 large ribs celery, julienned
1 large sweet red pepper, julienned
1 yellow pepper, julienned
Cornstarch

Combine all of the above ingredients, reserving the goose breast, and bring to a boil, stirring occasionally. Add the goose breast and simmer for 45 minutes. To thicken, mix cornstarch and water until well blended and gradually add to sauce. Bring to a boil, stirring constantly, until thickened. Reduce heat and simmer for an additional 15 minutes, stirring occasionally. Serve over cooked rice or noodles.

GOOSE AND RICE

2 goose breasts (approximately 4 cups) skinned, boned, and
   julienned
2 cups onions, sliced
4 cups carrots, julienned
2 cups celery, julienned
2 cups beef broth
2 cups burgundy
2 cups rice
2 tablespoons olive oil or butter
2 teaspoons salt
1/4 teaspoon pepper
6 to 8 stems saffron
2 tablespoons parsley

Saute' goose breasts in oil or butter. In five quart kettle, cook
celery, carrots, onions, parsley, saffron, salt, and pepper in two
cups of beef broth until tender. Combine goose breasts with
vegetables. Add rice and burgundy. Cover and simmer for
approximately 30 minutes.

GOOSE AND SAUERKRAUT

2 pounds goose breast, boned and skinned
2 pounds sauerkraut
1 cup water
2 onions, sliced
1 teaspoon black pepper
1 teaspoon Blackened Redfish Magic®
1/2 teaspoon Cajun seasoning

Combine all of the ingredients in a crock pot. Cook on high for eight hours. Serve with mashed potatoes.

PHEASANT CROQUETTES

4-1/2 cups pheasant breast, cooked, skinned, and boned
2 large eggs, hard boiled
3/4 cup minced onions
3/4 cup minced celery
1/4 cup minced red or yellow bell pepper
1 teaspoon minced garlic
3/4 teaspoon salt
1/4 teaspoon black pepper
1/8 teaspoon thyme
1/4 teaspoon paprika
2 tablespoons butter
2 tablespoons flour
1 cup milk
1 cup bread crumbs
2 large eggs, beaten

Dressing
3 cans cream of chicken soup
1 tablespoon lemon juice

Grind the pheasant and hard boiled eggs, using a fine grinding disk. Set aside. Cook onion, celery, pepper, and seasonings until vegetables are tender. In a large bowl, combine the ground

PHEASANT CROQUETTES (Continued)

pheasant, hard boiled eggs, and cooked vegetables. Prepare a white sauce using two tablespoons butter, two tablespoons flour, and one cup milk, salt and pepper, stirring constantly until thickened. Boil one minute. Chill. Add the chilled white sauce to the pheasant and vegetable mixture and form into croquettes. Dip croquettes in beaten eggs and then bread crumbs and pan fry in butter or oil until browned.

Combine the cream of chicken soup and lemon juice in a medium size sauce pan and bring to a boil. Spoon over croquettes to serve.

SMALL GAME

NOTES

PAN FRIED RABBIT

2 whole rabbits, cooked and boned
1 teaspoon salt
6 extra large eggs
1 teaspoon ground mustard
1 teaspoon onion powder
1/2 teaspoon black pepper
Saltine crackers, finely crushed
Flour
Butter or olive oil

Wisk together salt, eggs, mustard, onion powder, and black pepper. Place flour and cracker crumbs in separate bowls. Dredge rabbit pieces in flour, then egg mixture, then cracker crumbs and pan fry in a skillet in butter or olive oil until browned on both sides.

BAKED STUFFED RABBITS AND GRAVY

2 whole rabbits	Salt and pepper
2 cups water	Parsley flakes
Pinch of saffron	

Stuffing:

12 slices stale bread, cubed
1 cup chopped celery
1 cup chopped onions
1/2 teaspoon Blackened Redfish Magic®
1/2 teaspoon thyme
1/2 teaspoon black pepper
1 teaspoon salt
2 teaspoons ground mustard
1/4 teaspoon saffron, finely crumbled
2 tablespoons parsley flakes
4 tablespoons butter, softened
2 extra large eggs
Flour

In a large bowl, combine the above ingredients. Toss lightly with hands to avoid stuffing being too solid. Carefully place filling in cavity of each rabbit, front and top. To avoid filling being too

BAKED STUFFED RABBITS AND GRAVY (Continued)

solid, do not pack tightly. With needle and thread, loosely sew together. Place stuffed rabbits in a roasting pan. Sprinkle with salt, pepper, and parsley and add two cups of water. Bake covered at 350 degrees for two or two and one-half hours or until rabbits are soft and meat falls off the bones. Remove from roast pan and set aside.

Gravy:

Mix flour and cold water until well blended and gradually add to roast pan drippings. Bring to a boil, stirring constantly until thickened. Season to taste.

RABBIT AND WAFFLES

3 rabbits
3 cups water
2 teaspoons salt
Pinch of saffron

Cook until tender. Remove rabbits from kettle and strain broth.
Cut rabbit in small pieces and set aside. In a large sauce pan, add:

2 cups rabbit stock
1 cup water
3/4 cup chicken flavored gravy mix

Bring to a boil, stirring constantly, until thickened. Then add:

1/4 cup white wine
Salt to taste
1/4 teaspoon black pepper
1/2 teaspoon onion powder
1 tablespoon parsley
1 - 4 ounce can mushrooms, drained
4 cups rabbit

Stir together and simmer for 20 minutes. Thicken with flour and
serve over waffles.

FISH AND SEAFOOD

NOTES

COCKTAIL SAUCE

Combine the following ingredients:

2/3 cup ketchup
1 tablespoon hot sauce   (optional)
1/3 cup horseradish
1/8 teaspoon black pepper
1/4 teaspoon creole seasoning
1/4 teaspoon Blackened Redfish Magic®

MUSHROOMS STUFFED WITH CRAB MEAT

24 large mushrooms with centers removed
Stems and centers from mushrooms, chopped
1 medium onion, minced
2 tablespoons parsley flakes
2 tablespoons butter
1 teaspoon salt
1 teaspoon ground mustard
1 teaspoon crab and shrimp seasoning

1/4 teaspoon Old Bay® seasoning
1 tablespoon lemon juice
1/4 cup bread crumbs
1/4 cup mayonnaise
3/4 pound lump crab meat, thoroughly cleaned
Cheddar cheese crackers, finely crushed

Combine the mushroom stems, onions, parsley flakes, butter, and salt in a small skillet and saute' until onions are tender. Set aside to cool. In a large bowl, combine the remaining ingredients and then add the cooked mushroom stems. Stuff the crab mixture into mushroom caps and top with crumbs. Bake on a large greased cookie sheet at 350 degrees until crumbs are browned.

SCALLOPS AND FRESH WATER BASS GUMBO

2 pounds sea scallops
2 pounds fresh water bass, skinned and filleted
4 tablespoons olive oil or butter
2 cups chopped celery
2 cups chopped onions
3 cups sliced okra
1 cup chopped green or yellow bell pepper
1 teaspoon salt
1/2 teaspoon black pepper
1-1/2 teaspoons creole seasoning
2 teaspoons crab and shrimp seasoning
3 tablespoons parsley flakes
1 teaspoon minced garlic
1/8 cup sugar
1/2 cup Parmesan cheese
1 - 28 ounce can diced tomatoes
1 - 14.5 ounce can diced tomatoes
Flour

Saute' the scallops and bass in butter or olive oil. In a large kettle, combine the celery, onions, okra, peppers, and seasonings and cook in a little water until tender. Add the tomatoes, sugar, Parmesan cheese, scallops, and bass. Stir together. Simmer for 30 minutes. To thicken, mix flour and water until well blended and gradually add to gumbo. Bring to a boil, stirring constantly, until thickened. Serve over cooked rice.

BAKED SEAFOOD AU GRATIN

1/2 pound fresh water bass, skinned, boned, and cut in 2" cubes
1/2 pound medium size shrimp, cut in half
1/2 pound large scallops, cut in half
1/2 teaspoon crab and shrimp seasoning
1 tablespoon lemon juice
1/4 cup minced onions
3 tablespoons flour
3 tablespoons butter
1-1/4 cups milk
1/4 cup shredded sharp cheddar cheese
1 teaspoon salt
Paprika

In a medium skillet, saute' the bass, shrimp, scallops, seasoning, lemon juice, and onions. Prepare a white sauce with the butter, flour, and milk and gradually add cheese and salt. Bring to a boil, stirring constantly, until sauce thickens. Place seafood mixture in a greased casserole and cover with thickened cheese sauce. Sprinkle with paprika. Bake at 350 degrees uncovered for 45 minutes.

CRAB AU GRATIN

1 pound lump crab meat, thoroughly cleaned
1 teaspoon celery salt
1 tablespoon lemon juice
1 teaspoon crab and shrimp seasoning
1 teaspoon ground mustard
3 tablespoons butter
3 tablespoons flour
1-1/2 cups milk
1/2 cup sharp cheese, cubed
Cheddar cheese, shredded
Paprika

Place crab, celery salt, lemon juice, crab and shrimp seasoning, and mustard in a bowl. Stir together and set aside. Prepare a white sauce with the butter, flour, and milk, stirring constantly until thickened. Add cubed sharp cheese to the white sauce and stir until smooth. Combine the crab mixture and white sauce, mixing thoroughly. Pour into a greased casserole dish and top with cheese and paprika. Bake uncovered at 350 degrees for 30 minutes or until browned around the edges.

CRAB CAKES

1 pound lump crab meat, thoroughly cleaned
1 medium onion, minced
1 large rib celery, minced
2 large eggs, hard boiled and chopped
1 teaspoon salt
1/4 teaspoon black pepper
1/4 teaspoon Blackened Redfish Magic®
1 teaspoon ground mustard
1/4 teaspoon crab and shrimp seasoning
1 tablespoon parsley flakes
1/2 cup mayonnaise
3 ounces cream cheese
2/3 cup bread crumbs

Combine the crab meat, onion, celery, eggs, and seasonings. Add cream cheese and mayonnaise, mixing thoroughly. Add bread crumbs and form into cakes. Broil or pan fry in butter or oil until browned.

CRAB IMPERIAL

1 pound lump crab meat, thoroughly cleaned
2 jumbo eggs, hard boiled and chopped
3/4 cup minced onions
1/4 cup chopped celery
1/2 teaspoon salt
1/4 teaspoon Blackened Redfish Magic®
1/4 teaspoon Cajun seasoning
1/4 teaspoon crab and shrimp seasoning
3/4 teaspoon ground mustard
1 tablespoon lemon juice
1/3 cup mayonnaise
1 tablespoon butter
1 tablespoon flour
1/2 cup milk
Paprika
6 clam shells or small baking dishes

In a large bowl, combine the crab, eggs, onion, celery, seasonings, and mayonnaise. In a sauce pan, melt butter and blend in flour; add milk and stir constantly until boiling and thickened. Cool. Combine crab mixture with cooled white sauce and mix thoroughly. Spoon into clam shells, sprinkle with paprika, and place shells on a cookie sheet. Bake on middle rack at 350 degrees for 30 minutes or until lightly browned.

SEAFOOD LASAGNA

1 pound backfin lump crab meat, thoroughly cleaned
1 pound shrimp, cooked and halved
1 pound sea scallops, quartered
1 cup minced onions
1 tablespoon minced garlic
1/2 cup minced red or yellow bell pepper
1- 13-1/4 ounce can mushroom pieces
1 teaspoon oregano
1-1/2 teaspoons crab and shrimp seasoning
1 teaspoon Blackened Redfish Magic®
1 teaspoon thyme
1/2 teaspoon basil
1/2 teaspoon Cajun seasoning
1/2 teaspoon black pepper
1 - 12 ounce can tomato paste
2 - 28 ounce cans tomato puree
1 - 15 ounce can tomato sauce
1 cup Parmesan cheese
1-1/2 pounds ricotta cheese
1 pound mozzarella cheese, cubed
1/2 pound sharp cheese, shredded
1 - 8 ounce pack Oven Cooked Lasagna

SEAFOOD LASAGNA (Continued)

Place the crab meat, shrimp, scallops, onion, red or yellow pepper, mushrooms, seasonings, and tomatoes in a large kettle and mix thoroughly. Pour a small amount of the sauce in the bottom of two greased casserole dishes (9" x 13" x 2"). Layer lasagna, cheeses, and sauce, repeating until dishes are filled, ending with cheeses and sauce. Bake uncovered at 350 degrees for one hour and 15 minutes or until browned and bubbling.

BAKED BLUEFISH

1-1/2 pounds fresh bluefish
3/4 cup mayonnaise
1/4 cup sour cream
1 teaspoon ground mustard
1/4 teaspoon Old Bay® seasoning
1/4 teaspoon salt
1/4 teaspoon black pepper
1/4 teaspoon Blackened Redfish Magic®
1/4 cup white wine
1 tablespoon melted butter
1 tablespoon parsley flakes
Paprika

In a bowl, combine mayonnaise, sour cream, butter, and seasonings. Mix thoroughly. Set aside. Place fish in a 9" x 13" greased baking dish and pour mixture over fish. Sprinkle with paprika. Bake uncovered at 350 degrees for one hour.

FISH CAKES

1 pound kingfish, filleted and skinned
2 tablespoons butter
1 large onion, minced
1/4 cup minced celery
3 extra large eggs, hard boiled and finely chopped
1/4 teaspoon black pepper
1/4 teaspoon salt
1 tablespoon ground mustard
1/2 teaspoon Old Bay® seasoning
2 tablespoons parsley flakes
3/4 cup mayonnaise
1 tablespoon horseradish sauce
3/4 cup bread crumbs
Saltine crackers, crushed

Saute' fish, onions, celery, and seasonings in butter until tender, chopping fish with spatula as sauteing. Cool. Add hard boiled eggs, mayonnaise, horseradish sauce, and bread crumbs and mix thoroughly. Form into cakes, dredge in cracker crumbs, and pan fry.

FRIED FRESH WATER FISH

1-3/4 pounds fresh water fish, filleted
3 large eggs
1/4 teaspoon soy sauce
1/4 teaspoon Old Bay® seasoning
1/4 teaspoon Blackened Redfish Magic®
1/4 teaspoon onion powder
Cheddar cheese crackers, finely crushed

Place the eggs, soy sauce, Old Bay®, Blackened Redfish Magic®, and onion powder in a bowl and beat thoroughly. Dip fish in egg mixture and then into the cracker crumbs -- pat on both sides to keep the crumbs on the fish. Fry in butter and oil until browned on both sides.

FLOUNDER WITH WHITE SAUCE

2 pounds flounder fillets
1/2 pound large shrimp, cooked, peeled, and minced
4 tablespoons butter
4 tablespoons flour
1 cup milk
1 cup light cream
1/2 cup white wine
1 tablespoon lemon juice
1/2 teaspoon Blackened Redfish Magic®
1/4 teaspoon creole seasoning
1/2 teaspoon salt
1/4 teaspoon black pepper
Paprika

Place the flounder in a glass baking dish. Melt butter in a sauce pan and blend in flour. Slowly add milk and light cream and cook until thickened, stirring constantly.   Add the shrimp and remaining ingredients to the white sauce and stir together. Pour over fish and sprinkle with paprika. Bake uncovered at 350 degrees for 30 to 45 minutes or until sauce is browned and bubbling.

BAKED FISH WITH CHEESE SAUCE

1-1/2 pounds fish, skinned and filleted
4 tablespoons butter
4 tablespoons flour
2 cups milk
3/4 cup grated sharp cheese
1 teaspoon ground mustard
3/4 teaspoon salt
1/4 teaspoon black pepper
1 teaspoon lemon dill seasoning
1 tablespoon parsley flakes
1/4 teaspoon Old Bay® seasoning
Paprika

In a large sauce pan, melt butter and blend in flour. Slowly add milk, stirring constantly until mixture is thickened and boiling. Add cheese, mustard, salt, pepper, lemon dill seasoning, parsley flakes, and Old Bay® seasoning. Boil for one minute. Set aside. Place fish in a 9" x 13" greased baking dish and pour cheese sauce over fish. Sprinkle with paprika. Bake at 350 degrees for one hour or until browned and bubbling.

FISH OMELET

2 pounds fresh water fish, filleted and skinned
1/4 cup minced red bell pepper
1/2 cup minced onion
1-1/2 teaspoons salt
1/2 teaspoon black pepper
1/2 teaspoon minced garlic
2/3 tablespoon butter or oil
8 jumbo eggs
8 ounces sharp white cheddar cheese, shredded

In a large skillet, saute' fish, red pepper, onion, salt, pepper, and garlic until tender. Drain excess oil and break up fish into small pieces. Set aside. In a large bowl, beat eggs. Add cheese and remaining ingredients. Return to skillet and cook until omelet is fluffy and set.

HADDOCK IN CREAM SAUCE

2 pounds haddock, filleted
1 teaspoon yellow mustard
2 tablespoons lemon juice
1 tablespoon Worcestershire sauce
1 tablespoon salt
1/4 teaspoon pepper
1 teaspoon onion powder
3/4 teaspoon garlic powder
1 teaspoon garlic herb seasoning
2 tablespoons butter
1/2 pint light cream
1 tablespoon cornstarch
Paprika

Place the haddock in a greased baking dish. Combine the remaining ingredients and mix thoroughly. Pour the mixture over the fillets. Sprinkle with paprika. Bake uncovered at 350 degrees for 45 minutes or until browned and bubbling.

PAN FRIED FLOUNDER

1 pound flounder, filleted
Flour
4 large eggs
2 tablespoons mayonnaise
1 tablespoon lemon juice
1 teaspoon ground mustard
1/2 teaspoon Old Bay® seasoning
Salt and pepper to taste
Saltine crackers, finely crushed

In a bowl, beat eggs, mayonnaise, lemon juice, mustard, Old Bay® seasoning, salt, and pepper.   Dredge flounder in flour, egg mixture, and then cracker crumbs. Pan fry until golden brown on both sides.

SALMON CAKES

1 - 14.75 ounce can red or pink salmon
2 eggs, hard boiled and chopped
1 medium onion, chopped
1 tablespoon parsley
White sauce

Prepare white sauce as follows:
    2 tablespoons butter
    2 tablespoons flour
    1 tablespoon lemon juice
    3/4 cup milk
    Salt and pepper to taste

Over low heat, melt butter and add lemon juice. Stir in flour until blended. Gradually add milk, salt, and pepper and heat to boiling, stirring constantly. Boil approximately one minute or until mixture bubbles and thickens. Cool.

Combine the white sauce and the salmon, eggs, onions, and parsley. Mix thoroughly.

Form into cakes, roll lightly in bread crumbs, and pan fry. This can also be turned into a loaf pan and baked uncovered at 350 degrees for 45 minutes or until browned.

SALMON LOAF

1 - 14.75 ounce can red or pink salmon
3/4 cup minced onions
3/4 cup minced celery
1/4 cup minced green pepper
3 jumbo eggs, hard boiled and finely chopped
1/2 teaspoon salt
1/2 teaspoon Blackened Redfish Magic®
2 large eggs
2-1/2 cups bread crumbs
2 tablespoons mayonnaise
2 tablespoons butter
2 tablespoons flour
1 cup milk
Parsley flakes
Paprika

Over low heat, melt butter and stir in flour until blended. Gradually add milk, salt, and pepper and bring to boil, stirring constantly. Set aside to cool. Combine the remaining ingredients in a bowl and add the white sauce. Mix thoroughly and form a loaf. Place in a greased baking dish and sprinkle with paprika. Bake uncovered at 350 degrees for approximately 45 to 60 minutes or until browned.

SMOKED SALMON MELT

1/2 pound smoked salmon, flaked
3 large eggs, hard boiled and finely chopped
1 medium onion, minced
1/4 teaspoon crab and shrimp seasoning
1/2 teaspoon Blackened Redfish Magic®
1/4 teaspoon black pepper
1/2 teaspoon ground mustard
1/4 teaspoon paprika
Parsley flakes
4 ounces cream cheese
3/4 to 1 cup mayonnaise
Sharp cheese, sliced
Fresh tomatoes
Bread slices (with crusts removed) or English muffins

Combine salmon, hard boiled eggs, spices, cream cheese, and mayonnaise. Mix thoroughly. Place slice of cheese on bread, then tomato slice, salmon mixture, and top with cheese. Sprinkle with parsley flakes. Place on cookie sheet and bake at 350 degrees until bread or muffins are browned around the edges and cheese is melted.

This melt may be made with tuna, shrimp, crab, smoked fish, chicken, duck, pheasant.

PAN FRIED SHAD ROE

1 pair shad roe
2 large eggs, slightly beaten

Mix together:
    1 cup flour
    1 teaspoon salt
    1/4 teaspoon black pepper
    1/4 teaspoon Creole seasoning

Cracker crumbs

Dredge shad roe in flour mixture.   Dip in eggs and dredge in cracker crumbs. Pan fry in butter and/or oil very slowly until brown on both sides.

Serve with cocktail sauce.

SMOKED RAINBOW TROUT FISH CAKES

4 cups rainbow trout, ground
3 jumbo eggs, hard boiled and ground
1 cup chopped celery
1 cup chopped onions
1 cup diced potatoes
1 teaspoon salt
1/4 teaspoon black pepper
1/4 teaspoon thyme
1/2 teaspoon Blackened Redfish Magic®
1 teaspoon ground mustard
2 tablespoons parsley flakes
1 cup water
1/2 cup mayonnaise
Bread or cracker crumbs

Cook celery, onions, potatoes, and seasonings in a cup of water until tender. Cool. Combine trout, eggs, and the cooked ingredients in a large bowl. Add mayonnaise and mix thoroughly. Form into cakes and dredge in bread or cracker crumbs. Pan fry in butter and/or oil.

SMOKED SHAD CAKES

1 pound smoked shad, skinned, boned, and cut in small pieces
1 cup minced celery
1 cup minced onions
3 jumbo eggs, hard boiled and chopped
1/4 teaspoon Old Bay® seasoning
1/4 teaspoon creole seasoning
1/4 teaspoon crab and shrimp seasoning
1 teaspoon salt
1/4 teaspoon black pepper
1/2 cup mayonnaise
1/2 cup onion dip
3 ounces cream cheese
1/2 cup bread crumbs
White sauce:
    1 tablespoon butter
    1 tablespoon flour
    1/2 cup milk

Remove the dark meat of the fish and use the lighter meat. Combine all the ingredients in a large bowl. Prepare a white sauce by melting the butter and stirring in the flour to make a paste. Gradually add milk and stir constantly until boiling and thickened. Cool. Add the white sauce to the mixture and form into cakes. Pan fry until lightly browned on both sides.

HERRING PATTIES

1 pound herring
1 quart water
1 teaspoon salt
2 jumbo eggs, hard boiled
1/2 cup minced onions
1/4 cup minced green pepper
1/4 teaspoon black pepper
1/2 teaspoon crab and shrimp seasoning
1/2 teaspoon Blackened Redfish Magic®
1/2 teaspoon paprika
1/4 teaspoon thyme
1/2 teaspoon Cajun seasoning
1 tablespoon parsley flakes
1/2 cup unseasoned bread crumbs
1 cup mayonnaise
Saltine crackers, finely crushed

Place herring in a pressure cooker in water and salt and cook for
approximately one hour. If not using a pressure cooker, cook in a
kettle until bones are soft. Cool herring.

Grind herring and jumbo eggs, using a fine grinding disk, and add the
remaining ingredients. Mix thoroughly and form into patties.
Dredge in cracker crumbs. Pan fry in butter and oil until browned
on both sides.

BAKED STRIPED BASS

1-1/2 pounds striped bass, skinned and filleted
4 tablespoons butter
4 tablespoons flour
2 cups milk
1 teaspoon salt
1/4 teaspoon black pepper
1/4 teaspoon Blackened Redfish Magic®
1 tablespoon lemon juice
1 tablespoon parsley flakes
1/2 teaspoon onion powder
1/2 teaspoon garlic powder
Paprika

In a sauce pan, melt butter and slowly mix in flour; when blended together add milk, and remaining ingredients, stirring constantly until mixture is thickened and boiling. Boil for one minute. Set aside. Place fish in a 9" x 13" greased baking dish and pour white sauce over fish. Sprinkle with paprika. Bake uncovered at 350 degrees for 45 minutes, reduce heat to 300 degrees for about 10 or 15 minutes or until browned and bubbling.

Flounder, haddock, or any mild salt water fish may be used.

BROILED STRIPED BASS

2 pounds striped bass, filleted
3 tablespoons butter
1/2 teaspoon salt
1/2 teaspoon Blackened Redfish Magic®
1 tablespoon lemon juice
1 teaspoon ground mustard
1 - 6 ounce can mushroom soup
1 cup white wine
Paprika

Place fish in a buttered baking dish. In a medium size sauce pan, melt butter and add remaining ingredients. Mix well and pour over fish. Place under broiler until fish is white and tender and sauce is golden brown.

STUFFED STRIPED BASS

3 or 4 pounds striped bass, butterflied

Mix together:
3 cups plain bread crumbs
1 medium onion, minced
1 large rib celery, minced
1/3 small green or red pepper, minced
1 teaspoon ground mustard
1/8 teaspoon curry
1/2 teaspoon Blackened Redfish Magic®
1/4 teaspoon Old Bay® seasoning
1 teaspoon salt
1/4 teaspoon black pepper
1 tablespoon parsley flakes
4 ounce can mushroom pieces
1 jumbo egg

Place bass in a large greased baking dish with 1/4 cup water. Spoon the above mixture into the pocket of the fish. Dot with butter and sprinkle with paprika. Bake uncovered at 350 degrees for 45 minutes, reduce heat to 300 degrees for 15 minutes or until fish is browned around the edges.

STRIPED BASS WITH MUSTARD SAUCE

1 pound striped bass, filleted

Dredge fillets in flour. Pan fry in butter until brown on both sides.

Mix the following ingredients and serve over fried fillets.

1/2 cup yellow mustard
1/8 cup mayonnaise
1 tablespoon horseradish or 1 tablespoon horseradish sauce
1/8 teaspoon black pepper
1/4 teaspoon creole seasoning
1/4 teaspoon crab and shrimp seasoning
1/8 teaspoon ground red pepper   (optional)

This sauce can be used with any kind of fried or baked fish.

BAKED YELLOW FIN TUNA

2 pounds yellow fin tuna, skinned and boned
4 tablespoons butter
1 tablespoon lemon juice
1/2 teaspoon ground mustard
1/4 teaspoon Old Bay® seasoning
3/4 teaspoon salt
1/2 teaspoon minced garlic
1/4 cup water
Parsley flakes
Paprika

Melt butter and add lemon juice, mustard, Old Bay® seasoning, salt, and garlic. Mix thoroughly. Place tuna in greased baking dish with 1/4 cup water. Pour the butter mixture over tuna. Sprinkle with parsley and paprika. Bake at 350 degrees uncovered for 30 minutes.

VENISON

NOTES

DALE'S LASAGNA

2-1/4 pounds ground venison
2 medium onions, chopped
1 large red pepper, chopped
2 tablespoons crushed garlic
1 tablespoon salt
1/2 teaspoon black pepper
1 - 12 ounce can tomato paste
2 - 28 ounce cans tomato puree
3 - 15 ounce cans tomato sauce
2 tablespoons light brown sugar
1 teaspoon crushed oregano
2 tablespoons parsley flakes
3/4 teaspoon basil
1 - 8 ounce box Oven Ready Lasagna
1 pound ricotta cheese
8 ounce can Parmesan cheese
1 pound mozzarella cheese, cubed
1-1/2 cups white cheddar cheese, grated

Brown the first six ingredients in a large skillet until the onion and pepper are tender. In a large kettle, add the next seven ingredients and simmer. Combine tomato sauce and browned meat mixture and simmer for about 10 minutes. In two deep baking dishes (9" x 13" x 2"), alternate tomato/meat sauce, lasagna, and cheeses, repeating until dishes are filled, ending with sauce and cheeses on the top. Bake uncovered on middle oven rack at 350 degrees for about an hour or until brown and bubbly.

SHEPHERD'S PIE

1 pound ground venison
1 large onion, chopped
1 teaspoon garlic cloves, crushed
1 teaspoon salt
1/4 teaspoon pepper
2 cups water
2 packs brown gravy
6 large potatoes, cooked and mashed

Saute' the ground venison, onion, garlic, salt, and pepper in a large skillet. Combine gravy and water and wisk until smooth; cook for one minute. Combine gravy and browned venison mixture. Pour mixture into a glass baking dish and top with mashed potatoes. Bake uncovered at 350 degrees for 45 minutes or until brown and bubbling.

CHILI

1 pound ground venison
1 cup chopped onions
1/2 cup chopped green bell pepper
1/2 cup chopped celery
2 tablespoons minced garlic
1/4 teaspoon thyme
1/4 teaspoon crushed oregano
1/4 teaspoon ground red pepper   (optional)
1/4 teaspoon salt
1/4 teaspoon black pepper
2 tablespoons parsley flakes
1 - 28 ounce can diced tomatoes
1 cup tomato puree
2 tablespoons light brown sugar
1 tablespoon vinegar
1 tablespoon chili powder
2 - 14 ounce cans red kidney beans

Saute' the first eleven ingredients in a large skillet until browned. Add the remaining ingredients and stir. Simmer one hour, stirring occasionally.

PIZZA

1/2 pound ground venison
1/4 cup minced onion
1/4 cup minced broccoli
1/4 cup minced green pepper
1 - 14 ounce can pizza sauce
8 ounce pack mozzarella cheese, shredded
6 ounce can sliced mushrooms
Pepperoni
14" pizza crust

Preheat oven to 425 degrees.

Saute' first four ingredients in skillet.   Add sauce.   Spread on
pizza crust.   Add cheese, mushrooms, and top with pepperoni.
Place pizza on stone or cookie sheet and place on bottom oven
rack. Bake at 425 degrees 15 to 20 minutes or until edges of crust
are brown and cheese is bubbling.

BURGERS ON THE GRILL

1 pound ground venison
1 large leek, minced
1/4 cup minced celery
1/4 cup grated carrots
1 extra large egg
1/2 teaspoon salt
1/4 teaspoon black pepper
1 tablespoon parsley flakes
1/4 teaspoon Blackened Redfish Magic®
1 tablespoon soy sauce
1 - 14 ounce can whole tomatoes, drained
2 small cans mushrooms, drained
3/4 teaspoon minced garlic
Bread crumbs

Combine all ingredients in a large mixing bowl. Mix together to form patties. Grill thoroughly until browned on both sides.

SALISBURY STEAK

1 pound ground venison
1/2 pound lean ground beef
1 large onion, finely chopped
2 large celery ribs, finely chopped
1 - 14.5 ounce can crushed tomatoes, drained
1 large egg
1 teaspoon minced garlic
1 teaspoon salt
1/4 teaspoon black pepper
3 packs brown gravy mix
1 cup water
1 - 14 ounce can beef broth
3/4 cup burgundy or red wine

Place the venison, beef, onion, celery, tomatoes, egg, garlic, salt, and pepper in a large mixing bowl and mix well. Form into patties. Saute' in frying pan until lightly browned on both sides. In a saucepan, combine the gravy mix, water, and beef broth, bring to a boil, stirring constantly. Add the burgundy and pour entire mixture over the sauteed patties. Simmer for 30 minutes.

CROCK POT TENDERLOIN

2 to 3 pounds venison tenderloin
1 - 14 ounce can beef broth
3 packs brown gravy
3 cups water
3 beef bouillon cubes
1 tablespoon crushed garlic
1 large onion, sliced
1 medium red pepper, chopped
1 medium yellow pepper, chopped
1 - 6 ounce can sliced mushrooms
1 tablespoon soy sauce

Mix all the ingredients together, reserving the venison tenderloin.
Pour into crock pot. Add tenderloin and cook on high for about
eight hours. To thicken, mix cornstarch and water until blended.
Add gradually to broth and cook on low for 30 minutes.

CROCK POT STROGANOFF

1-1/2 pounds venison steak, cut in one inch strips
1 - 14 ounce can beef broth
3 packs beef gravy
3 cups water
3/4 cup red wine
2 beef bouillon cubes
1 teaspoon crushed garlic
1 large onion, chopped
1 small green pepper, chopped
1 can sliced mushrooms
4 tablespoons sour cream

Combine the beef broth, gravy, water, and wine in a crock pot. Mix thoroughly and add the remaining ingredients, reserving the sour cream. Start on high for about three hours, reducing heat to low for five to six hours or until meat is tender. Just before serving, stir in the sour cream. Serve over cooked noodles.

ROAST

2 or 3 pounds venison roast
1 - 48 ounce can beef broth
3 packs brown gravy
1 pack onion soup
1 large onion, chopped
1 - 6 ounce can whole mushrooms
2 large carrots cut in chunks
3 large potatoes, peeled and quartered

Combine the beef broth, gravy, onion soup, and chopped onions in a large roasting pan. Place venison roast in pan and baste roast with mixture. Place mushrooms, carrots and potatoes around roast. Roast at 350 degrees for approximately 3 hours or until tender. Gravy can be served over potatoes and carrots.

MEATBALLS

1/2 pound ground venison
1/2 cup plain bread crumbs
1/2 small green pepper, minced
1 medium onion, minced
1 large egg
1 tablespoon garlic powder
1/4 teaspoon black pepper
1 tablespoon vinegar
1 tablespoon yellow mustard
1 cup sharp cheese, finely shredded
1 tablespoon oil
3 packs brown gravy mix
3 cups water
1/4 cup red wine
1/2 cup flour

Combine venison, bread crumbs, pepper, onion, egg, garlic powder, pepper, vinegar, mustard, and cheese. Mix well. Shape into small balls. Dredge balls in flour. Saute' meatballs in oil or butter, being careful to brown evenly. In sauce pan, add gravy, water and wine, stirring constantly until boiling. Pour over meatballs and simmer 30 minutes. Serve over cooked noodles.

MEATBALLS

1 pound ground venison
1 large onion, minced
1/8 cup minced green or red pepper
1 large egg
1 tablespoon parsley flakes
1 teaspoon minced garlic
1/4 teaspoon thyme
1 tablespoon vinegar
1/4 teaspoon black pepper
1 - 14.5 ounce can crushed tomatoes
1 cup bread crumbs
1/2 cup flour

Combine the above ingredients, reserving the flour. Mix thoroughly. Form into small balls, dredge in flour, and brown. Excellent served with spaghetti sauce.

ROASTED TENDERLOIN CUBES AND GRAVY

2 pounds venison loin, cut in 1" cubes
1 medium onion, chopped
1 cup fresh mushrooms, chopped
1/2 teaspoon minced garlic
3 tablespoons butter or olive oil
2 packs brown gravy mix
1 pack onion soup mix
1-1/2 cups water
1/4 cup burgundy or red wine

Saute' the tenderloin cubes, onion, mushrooms, and garlic in butter or olive oil until browned. In a sauce pan, combine the gravy and onion soup mixes together with water and burgundy or wine, and stir well; bring to a boil for one minute. Place tenderloin cubes in a small roasting pan and cover with gravy mixture. Bake at 350 degrees for about 45 minutes or until cubes are tender. Serve over noodles or rice.

SAUSAGE

7 pounds lean ground venison
3 pounds lean ground pork
2 cups water
1-1/2 tablespoons onion powder
1 tablespoon garlic powder
1-1/2 tablespoons coarse black pepper
5 tablespoons coarse salt
1 tablespoon Blackened Redfish Magic®
1 tablespoon ground mustard
2 teaspoons thyme
1/2 teaspoon ground red pepper (optional)
Hog casings

Place venison and pork in a large container and add the remaining
ingredients. Mix thoroughly. Place mixture in a sausage
stuffer and stuff into hog casings. If you don't have a sausage
stuffer, this mixture can be made into patties and can be pan fried
or grilled.

HOT ROAST VENISON SANDWICHES

1 pound left over venison roast, finely cut
4 packs brown gravy mix
3 cups water
1 teaspoon garlic powder or 1 tablespoon crushed garlic
1 teaspoon onion powder
1 teaspoon dried parsley
1 cup fresh cleaned and sliced mushrooms or
    1 - 8 ounce can sliced mushrooms
1/2 cup burgundy

Combine gravy mix, water, garlic, onion powder, and parsley in a sauce pan. Stir constantly until boiling. Add the mushrooms, burgundy, and cut up venison roast. Simmer 10 minutes. Serve over sliced bread.

MEATLOAF

1-1/2 pounds ground venison
1/2 pound lean ground beef
2 large onions, minced
2 large celery ribs, finely chopped
1 medium green pepper   (optional)
1 - 14.5 can peeled, crushed tomatoes, drained
2 large eggs
1 teaspoon salt
1/4 teaspoon black pepper
1 teaspoon ground mustard
1/2 teaspoon chili powder
2 tablespoons parsley flakes
3/4 cup ketchup
1/2 cup bread crumbs

Mix the above ingredients together, reserving the ketchup. Form into a loaf and place in roasting pan. Spread ketchup on top of loaf.   Bake covered at 350 degrees for about 1 hour. Remove cover and bake for about 30 minutes.

MEATLOAF WITH BREAD FILLING

2 pounds ground venison
2 large onions, finely chopped
1 medium red pepper, finely chopped
2 large ribs celery, finely chopped
1 small carrot, grated
1 tablespoon soy sauce
2 tablespoons yellow mustard
1 tablespoon salt
1 teaspoon black pepper
1 tablespoon Worcestershire sauce
2 large eggs
1 - 28 ounce can crushed tomatoes
Bread filling*

Mix ingredients in large bowl and add one-half can crushed tomatoes and mix thoroughly. Spray bottom of roasting pan with cooking spray. Place half of the meat mixture in the roast pan, add bread filling, and remaining meat mixture, shaping into a loaf. Pour remaining crushed tomatoes over the loaf and bake at 350 degrees for 90 minutes, then reduce heat to 300 degrees for 30 minutes.

*Refer to bread filling recipe.

CHEESE LOAF

1 pound ground venison
1 pound ground sirloin or ground pork
1 cup chopped onions
1/3 cup finely chopped green pepper
1 cup finely chopped celery
1-1/2 tablespoons salt
1/2 teaspoon black pepper
2 large eggs
1 teaspoon ground mustard
1- 14.5 ounce can diced tomatoes, drained
1 cup plain bread crumbs
1 - 8 ounce pack white cheddar cheese, shredded
3/4 cup ketchup
Parsley

Mix the above ingredients together, reserving half the can of tomatoes, and form into a loaf. Place in a greased roasting pan, pour the remaining tomatoes over the loaf, and top with ketchup and parsley. Bake at 350 degrees for 2-1/2 to three hours or until nicely browned.

VENISON/BEEFSTICKS

NOTES

VENISON STICKS

2-1/2 pounds ground venison
1 pound ground sirloin or 1 pound ground lean pork
1 tablespoon plain salt (not iodized)
1 tablespoon Tender Quick® meat cure or 1 tablespoon plain salt
1 cup light brown sugar
1 tablespoon onion powder
1 tablespoon garlic powder
1 teaspoon Blackened Redfish Magic®
1 teaspoon black pepper
1-1/4 teaspoons ground red pepper
        (3 teaspoons if you prefer it hotter)
1 teaspoon paprika
1 tablespoon ground mustard
1 tablespoon soy sauce
1 tablespoon liquid smoke
1 cup shredded sharp cheese (optional)

Combine all of the above ingredients in a large container. Mix
thoroughly. Place in the refrigerator at least 8 hours to cure. If
you have a sausage stuffer, use medium size tube and pack meat
in tightly. You do not need a casing as you can form the sticks out
on your hand approximately eight to ten inches long or any
desired size.   You can also form into squares by placing on
a cookie sheet and pressing flat with the palm of your hand.

VENISON STICKS (Continued)

Use a pizza cutter to cut into squares, remove with a thin spatula, and place on racks or drain grates.   Set oven temperature to 150 degrees. Keep oven door ajar approximately four inches. Place foil on bottom oven rack (loosely along sides, front, and back so heat can circulate in oven) to catch drippings. After one hour remove foil. It usually takes between 6 to 8 hours or until sticks are solid. Do not over dry.

This can also be done in a smoker with or without chips.

JERKY

NOTES

JERKY

6 pounds venison roast (or any other game, fowl or large animals)
3 teaspoons garlic powder
6 teaspoons onion powder
6 teaspoons meat tenderizer
1-1/2 teaspoons black pepper
2 teaspoon ground mustard
2 cups soy sauce
2 cups Worcestershire sauce
1-1/2 cup burgundy or red wine
6 teaspoons liquid smoke
1 teaspoon Blackened Redfish Magic®

Semi-freeze venison roast for easier slicing. Slice into 1/4" thick strips about 2" wide and 3" to 4" long. Combine all of the above ingredients in a large bowl. Mix thoroughly and then add venison strips. Marinate in brine 24 hours, turning meat occasionally. Drain brine and place strips on paper towels. Pat dry. Place in oven, dehydrator or smoker. If using oven, place strips on draining grates and set oven temperature to 150 degrees and keep the oven door open approximately four inches. Place foil on bottom of oven (loosely along sides, front, and back so heat can circulate in oven) to catch drippings. After one hour remove foil. Check in three hours, some pieces may be done, although it usually takes between 6 to 8 hours. Pieces should be chewy, not brittle.

MISCELLANEOUS

NOTES

BREAD STUFFING

12 slices stale bread, cubed
3 large eggs
2 large ribs celery, finely chopped
1 large onion, chopped
1 tablespoon parsley flakes
1 teaspoon salt
1/4 teaspoon black pepper
5 tablespoons softened butter

In a large bowl, combine all the above ingredients. Toss lightly with your hands until ingredients are mixed together. Place in a greased baking dish, being careful not to pack stuffing tightly in dish, and bake covered at 350 degrees for 45 minutes. Uncover and bake for 15 minutes.

This can also be used for stuffing in fowl or game birds.

OYSTER FILLING

4 dozen medium size oysters
3/4 cup oyster broth
1/2 teaspoon Blackened Redfish Magic®
1/2 teaspoon creole seasoning
1-1/2 teaspoons salt
1/4 teaspoon black pepper
1 cup minced onions
1 cup chopped celery
12 slices stale bread, cubed

In a large bowl, combine all of the above ingredients. Pour into a buttered baking dish. Dot with butter. Place in oven and bake uncovered at 350 degrees for about one hour or until top is lightly browned.

WHITE SAUCE

2 tablespoons butter
2 tablespoons flour
1 cup milk
1 teaspoon salt
Dash of pepper

Melt butter. Stir in flour with wire wisk until well blended. Gradually stir in milk, salt, and pepper and heat to boiling, stirring constantly. Boil approximately one minute or until mixture is thick and smooth.

If you prefer a thinner white sauce, use 2 cups of milk.

You can vary the taste by adding lemon, dill, cheese, or any seasoning your prefer.

INDEX

NOTES

INDEX

INDEX

INDEX

INDEX

NOTES

SMOKING IN A GAS GRILL

If a smoker is not available, it is possible to use a large gas grill.

1. Remove grill grate.
2. Place wood chips in foil and fold foil loosely, leaving a small opening at the top.
3. Place foil on lava rocks or steel bottom of grill.
4. Turn left burner on high and close top of grill. It will take approximately 15 or 20 minutes for the wood chips to start smoking.
5. Remove fish or fowl from brine and transfer to a two-sided fish or burger rack, securely fastening the top so whatever you are smoking will not fall out.
6. Place rack on top, right side on the warming rack.
7. Turn burner to low and close top.
8. Check in approximately one hour — fish should be done, however, fowl would probably take a little longer.

FOWL MUST ALWAYS BE COOKED AFTER SMOKING.

ORDER FORM

Original Wild Game, Fish, and Seafood Recipes

Please send check or money order in the amount of $20.00
Plus $5.00 for tax, shipping and handling to:

DALE L. SHELLY
P.O. BOX 6070
WYOMISSING, PA   19610

Please forward_____copies of:
Original Wild Game, Fish, and Seafood Recipes to:

Name: _____

Mailing Address: _____

City: _____

State: _____

Zip: _____

Phone: _____

Credit Card: [ ] Visa   [ ] Master Card

Number: _____

Expiration Date: _____

CVV Code _____

(CVV code is found on the back of your credit card, last 3 numbers.)

Enclosed is my check/money order in the amount of $_____

You are here by authorized to charge my credit
card in the amount of $_____

Signature_____
(Signature required for credit card orders.)
Or call 610-375-7925 to place your order by phone!